Proceedings of the 7th
University House Wine Symposium

Proceedings of the 7th
University House Wine Symposium

Edited by Kiaran Kirk and John Richards

UNIVERSITY
HOUSE

Published by ANU eView
The Australian National University
Canberra ACT 0200, Australia
Email: enquiries.eview@anu.edu.au

This title is also available online at http://eview.anu.edu.au

---

National Library of Australia Cataloguing-in-Publication entry

Author: Wine Symposium (7th : 2012 : Australian National University)

Title: Proceedings of the 7th University House Wine Symposium / edited by Kiaran Kirk and John Richards.

ISBN: 9781921934025 (pbk.) 9781921934032 (ebook)

Subjects: Wine and wine making--Australia--Congresses.

Other Authors/Contributors:
          Kirk, Kiaran.
          Richards, John.

Front cover photo: William Wang

Back cover photo: Stuart Hay

Dewey Number: 641.220994

All rights reserved. No part of this publication may be reproduced, stored in a retrieval system or transmitted in any form or by any means, electronic, mechanical, photocopying or otherwise, without the prior permission of the publisher.

Cover design and layout by ANU eView

This edition © 2012 ANU eView

Contents

Foreword vii

1. History of the University House Wine Symposia 1
   John Richards

2. Pioneers of the Canberra District 3

3. The Organising and Program Committees 5

4. The Symposium Program 7

5. The Seventh Wine Symposium Poem: *Chateau Mary Celeste* 9
   Chris Clarke

6. The 7th University House Wine Symposium Gala Dinner. 11

7. Climate Controversies and Varietal Views: The papers
   of the Seventh University House Wine Symposium 13
   Kiaran Kirk

8. Opening Speech 17
   Ian Young

9. Projected Climate: Means and extremes. How will this
   impact the wine industry? 19
   Leanne Webb

10. A Brief History of the Canberra District 35
    Brian Johnston

11. Riesling: The noblest white. 41
    Brian Croser

12. Shiraz: Past, present and future. 51
    Dan Buckle

13. Emerging and Alternative Varieties: Considerations,
    challenges and choices. 59
    Libby Tassie

14. Great Australian Wine: Are there any alternatives? 69
    Nick Stock

15. The Search for Consistency or the Pursuit of Excellence?
    Single vineyard, regional and multi-regional as winemaking
    choices in Australia 73
    Brian Walsh

Foreword

The Seventh University House Wine Symposium was held at the House on 20 and 21 May 2011. These proceedings record the events that made up the symposium and include copies of the papers delivered by the invited speakers.

The symposium was planned to coincide with the fortieth anniversary of the first plantings in the modern era of winemaking in the Canberra District. While academic in its prime purpose, the event also served as a celebration of the achievements of those pioneers who undertook the initial plantings of the first wineries that today comprise the district, as well as those of the many that followed. Together they have established the district as one that has a significant and fast-growing reputation, both nationally and internationally.

There were two interleaved themes for the symposium: the wines and grape varieties of the Canberra District and the potential impact of climate change on the local and national wine industry. There was a full day of talks, with the organising committee choosing a range of speakers and discussants with a stimulating (and sometimes provocative) range of views on climate change, and on the grape varieties that might be best suited to the district. A wine-tasting in the hall—thought to be the largest and most comprehensive event of its type ever held in Canberra—featured offerings from 33 of the local wineries. A gala dinner showcased ten of the region's best wines, selected for the occasion by two noted wine judges, Nick Stock and Nick Bullied, from samples tendered by local wineries, as well as featuring a talk from Australia's pre-eminent wine writer, James Halliday.

The symposium also included a series of visits to local wineries at which the winemakers themselves spoke of their production techniques and varieties, providing tastings from the barrel or from the cellar of wines that in some cases were not available to the general public. Those who took part in the tours commented very favourably on how they supplemented the lecture and wine-tasting components of the symposium.

Central to the symposium was the launch by the ACT Minister for Tourism and Deputy Chief Minister, Andrew Barr, of the second edition of *Wines of the Canberra District* by Brian Johnston and Janet Johnson.

The success of the symposium was very much the result of the efforts of a dedicated and highly engaged organising committee and program committee, including representation from both the University and the local industry.

The memberships of these committees can be found on page 5. The smooth running of the event also owed a great deal to the staff of University House; their efforts were very much appreciated by all involved.

Professor Kiaran Kirk,
Chair,
Organising Committee

Professor John Richards,
Master

1. History of the University House Wine Symposia

John Richards

Two years before University House opened on 16 February 1954 a wine committee had been formed, recognising the longstanding association between fine wines and the House (Waterhouse 2005). Wine-tastings were popular events at the House from the very early days, as were wine-bottlings.

On 26 and 27 October 1956, the First Wine Symposium of University House was held at the instigation of the foundation Master, Professor Dale Trendall. It had a focus on Australian wines and winegrowing regions, and was organised by Professor John Lovering, then of the Research School of Earth Sciences.[1]

The second symposium, which is thought to have been one of the most successful events under Trendall's mastership, was held on 1 and 2 September 1967—again with the theme of Australian wines. So successful was the event that Trendall's initiative drew major praise from Sir Leonard Huxley, the then Vice-Chancellor of The Australian National University.

At the third symposium in August 1979—sometimes referred to as the Silver Jubilee wine symposium—during the mastership of Professor Ralph Elliott, an image of an Ancient Greek drinking cup, brought to the House by Trendall as part of a representative collection of Greek attic cups and vases, was chosen as the logo for the symposium. The role of drawing the cup fell to Richard Barwick, who was a member of the organising committee for the second and third symposia and was on the committee for the seventh. The cup logo used for that symposium was subsequently adopted by Elliott as the now well-known symbol for University House. The symposium was opened by His Excellency the Governor-General, Sir Zelman Cowen, and the after-dinner speaker at the symposium banquet was the late Len Evans, well-known winemaker, writer and critic.

The sixth symposium was held in November 1994, on the theme of wines of the southern hemisphere. Organised by the then Master, Dr Rafe de Crespigny, it featured speakers from Chile, Argentina, South Africa and New Zealand, as well as from Australia. The inaugural Helmut Becker Lecture, entitled 'The

---

[1] Scans of the proceedings of the 1956, 1967, 1979 and 1994 symposia are available at University House and can be read on its website.

wine cannot be better than the grape', was presented at dinner by Dr John Possingham, then Chief Scientist of CSIRO's Institute of Plant Production and Processing.

Records for the fourth and fifth symposia are less clear; both seem to have been run under the auspices of the University, but not at University House. The brochure for Wine Talk '84, held in November 1984 at the ANU Staff Centre (at one stage part of University House) refers to a previous event in 1979—curiously close to the Third University House Symposium. The 1984 event coincided with the 1984 National Wine Show and so was able to take advantage of a number of key figures visiting Canberra, including Wolf Blass, Max Schubert, Murray Tyrrell and Edgar Reik.

The Seventh University House Wine Symposium was held on 20 and 21 May 2011 to coincide with the fortieth anniversary of the first commercial plantings in the modern era of Canberra and district winemaking. Like its predecessors, it featured lectures on contemporary themes, including the likely effects of a changing climate on winemaking. It concluded with a gala dinner in the Hall of University House at which the best of Canberra's wines were on show.

Reference

Waterhouse, Jill, 2004, *University House As They Experienced It, A History 1954–2004*, University House, Canberra.

2. Pioneers of the Canberra District

The Seventh University House Wine Symposium coincided with the fortieth anniversary of the establishment of the first of the now more than 30 commercial wineries and more than 150 vineyards that make up the Canberra District. The district is recognised, both nationally and internationally, as one of Australia's significant cool-climate wine regions, and the organising committee for the symposium was delighted that three of the district's pioneers—John Kirk, Edgar Riek and Ken Helm—were able to attend the symposium as guests of honour.

John Kirk established Clonakilla in the Murrumbateman area in 1971, planting several different varieties and, in 1976, selling the first commercial wines to be produced in the Canberra District in the modern era. Clonakilla produces a range of wines, with the Shiraz and, in particular, the Shiraz-Viognier blend—pioneered by John's son Tim, now Clonakilla's CEO and Chief Winemaker—being the flagship for the winery, and to some extent for the district as a whole.

Also in 1971, Edgar Riek established his vineyard at the edge of Lake George and, over the following years, planted a wide range of varieties. Wine was produced initially under the Cullarin Cellars label, and, later, in the early 1980s, under the Lake George label. The Lake George Winery has now changed hands, but continues to make wine from some of the oldest vines in the district.

In 1973 Ken Helm, with his wife, Judith, established Helm Wines in the Murrumbateman area, and it has forged an outstanding reputation for Riesling and Cabernet Sauvignon in particular. Ken himself has been a passionate advocate for Riesling, locally, nationally and internationally, instigating the Canberra International Riesling Challenge, which is held annually and is the largest competition of its kind in the southern hemisphere.

John Kirk, Ken Helm and Edgar Riek

3. The Organising and Program Committees

Organising Committee

Kiaran Kirk (Chair), ANU
Richard Barwick, ANU
Colin Steele, former librarian, ANU
Anne Caine, Lerida Estate Winery
Janet Johnson, McKellar Ridge Wines
Brian Johnston, McKellar Ridge Wines
Walter Sauer, General Manager, UH
Lyn North, Functions Manager, UH
Deane Terrell, ANU and Quarry Hill
John Richards, Master, UH
Catriona Jackson, Communications, ANU
Ashley Zmijewski, Marketing, ANU

Program Committee

Tim Kirk, Clonakilla
Kiaran Kirk, ANU
Deane Terrell, ANU and Quarry Hill
Brian Schmidt, ANU and Maipenrai
Catriona Jackson, ANU

4. The Symposium Program

Friday, 20 May 2011

Common Room

8:30 am	Registration, Hall Foyer, University House
9:00 am	Welcome and Opening, *Ian Young*
9:10 am	A Brief History of the Canberra Wine District, *Brian Johnston*
9:30 am	Formal Launch of *Wines of the Canberra District: Coming of Age*, *Andrew Barr*
9:50 am	Climate Change and its Local Effects in Australia, *Andrew Pitman*
10:20 am	Morning Tea
10:50 am	Projected Climate: Means and extremes. How will this impact the wine industry? *Leanne Webb*
11:20 am	Riesling: The noblest wine, *Brian Croser*
12:00 pm	Shiraz: Past, present and future, *Dan Buckle*
12:40 pm	Lunch
2:00 pm	Alternative 2.0—New varieties and working titles, *Nick Stock*
2:40 pm	Alternative and Emerging Varieties: Considerations, challenges and choices, *Libby Tassie*
3:10 pm	The Search for Consistency or the Pursuit of Excellence? Single vineyard, regional and multi-regional as winemaking choices in Australia, *Brian Walsh*
3:50 pm	Afternoon Tea
4:20 pm	Q & A and Panel Discussion, *moderated by Nick Stock*
5:30 pm	Close
6:00 pm	Wine-Tasting

Proceedings of the 7th University House Wine Symposium

Saturday, 21 May 2011

10:00 am – 4:00 pm Winery tours

Tour 1
McKellar Ridge Wines
Eden Road Wines
Clonakilla Wines
Four Winds Vineyard

Tour 2
Capital Wines
Yarrh Wines
Helm Wines
Collector Wines

Tour 3
Pankhurst Wines
Gallagher Wines
Jeir Creek Wines
Brindabella Hills Winery

Tour 4
Mount Majura Vineyard
Shepherds Run
Lerida Estate Wines
Lark Hill Winery

Symposium Gala Dinner

7:00 pm   Pre-dinner drinks, Common Room
7:30 pm   Dinner, Hall, *Guest Speaker: James Halliday*

5. The Seventh Wine Symposium Poem: *Chateau Mary Celeste*

Chris Clarke

My youth has now departed, once I knew
The subtle secrets of each local brew,
The latest from the Wig and Pen, and more
Where I could cadge it from the home-brew door.
But knowing aught of wine was still ahead
Due to the lack of what was known as 'bread'.
And yet there was that day pre-GPS
A party of us cruising round by guess,
Behind a hill, up dirt tracks, past a gate
Had stumbled on a vineyard. Being late
We called in for directions home, but found
No living soul, though wonders all around:
The vibrant vines up almost to the roof,
Cellar vats marked 'Eighteen per cent proof'
And open sample bottles. We were dry
And though we found no owner, stayed to try.
We left in darkness, well before the days
When breathalysers modified our ways.
We dubbed the place 'Chateau Mary Celeste',
And boxed the compass, north, east, south and west,
We asked around, searched maps, and drove in hope
But never found our way back to that slope.
And still it haunts me, half-remembered labels,
Weird names, and linen cloths on tables,
Menus like a restaurant, and views
Across the Brindies' late-hour shaded blues.
Had we come across the very first
Of many now that slake a classy thirst?
Custodian of the Arts Grants, hear my plea

And see your way to bankrolling for me
A research project on the local wines
That I may find what origin defines
Our vintners' art, the soils and the clime
And render it in metre, and in rhyme.
And maybe, if the Powers see the jest,
Find traces of Chateau Mary Celeste.

6. The 7th University House Wine Symposium Gala Dinner

THE 7TH UNIVERSITY HOUSE
WINE SYMPOSIUM

Gala Dinner
Saturday 21 May 2011

University House
The Australian National University
1 Balmain Cres Acton ACT
02 6125 5270 or 02 6125 5271
www.anu.edu.au/unihouse/winesymposium

Menu

Tuna Tataki brochette with dukka spice and aioli
Corn cake blini with house smoked chicken, chili jam & thyme
Brioche toast with rallegio & glazed pear

2008 Lark Hill Méthode Champenoise Rosé "Blanc Du Noir"

Welcome by Prof John Richards
Master, University House

Capsicum & tomato broth with crab & avocado timbale,
finished with micro herbs

2009 Eden Road 'The Long Road' RHE
2010 Helm Wines Premium Riesling
2006 Shepherd's Run Riesling

Oriana Chorale

Dry aged local rib eye fillet of beef, vine ripened tomato farci,
beetroot roesti, asparagus spears & porcini mushroom jus

or

Yarra Valley organic free range chicken breast fillet,
fig & brandy stuffing, vine ripened tomato farci,
beetroot roesti, asparagus spears & thyme pan jus

or

Cinnamon rubbed Gressingham duck breast fillet, vine ripened
tomato farci, beetroot roesti, asparagus spears & mandarin jus

2008 Maipenrai Pinot Noir
2010 Ravensworth Sangiovese
2009 Clonakilla Shiraz Viognier

Address by James Halliday

Selection of Australian cheese with
macerated fruits and muscatels

2008 Collector Reserve Shiraz
2009 Mount Majura Vineyard TSG

Reading of the Symposium Poem
Chateau Marie Céleste
by Chris Clarke

Trio of desserts

Coconut & lemongrass pannacotta with lime,
chili & orange syrup, almond tuille

and

Pear & almond frangipani tart with Frangelico syrup

and

Gingerbread ice cream

2007 Lerida Estate Botrytis Pinot Gris

Coffee or tea with a selection of truffles

We are grateful to Nick Bullied & Nick Stock who selected the wines for
tonight's dinner from among the best wines of the Canberra District

7. Climate Controversies and Varietal Views: The papers of the Seventh University House Wine Symposium

Kiaran Kirk

The Seventh University House Wine Symposium opened with the focus firmly on climate change. Brian Schmidt, a vigneron with a passion for Pinot Noir (and who was, later that year, awarded the Nobel Prize for Physics), introduced the first speaker of the day, Professor Andy Pitman. Andy is Professor in Climate Science at the University of New South Wales and Director of the Australian Research Council (ARC) Centre of Excellence for Climate System Science. He presented data showing climate change trends and he emphasised the need for planning for climate change and for investing in adaptation, noting that there is no 'silver bullet'. He also spoke passionately about the nature of the climate change debate. Andy's other commitments precluded him from providing a written paper for the proceedings, but aspects of what he covered in his symposium talk are included in articles posted on the ARC Centre's website (<http://www.climatescience.org.au/articles/peerreview.html>). In the best traditions of academic meetings, Andy's talk generated a lot of discussion that continued throughout the symposium and beyond. The following evening, in his talk at the symposium dinner, James Halliday, the foremost observer of and commentator on the Australian wine scene, took the opportunity to respond to aspects of Andy's talk and to take issue with the extent of human-induced climate change. This in turn led to further discussion and debate in articles in *The Canberra Times*, both by Brian Schmidt (who urged people to read the Australian Academy of Science's report *The Science of Climate Change* (2010)) and by wine writer Chris Shanahan (2011), as well as on Brian Croser's Tapanappa Wine website blog (2011).

The second speaker at the symposium was Leanne Webb, a research fellow at the University of Melbourne and CSIRO, whose work is in the field of climate change adaptation, with a particular focus on the wine industry. In her article for these proceedings, Leanne focuses on climate projections for Australia, and the Canberra District in particular, discussing the likely magnitude of the temperature increase, and the possible consequences in terms of rainfall and extreme temperature events. Leanne then goes on to provide a thoughtful analysis of the likely impacts of climate change on grape growing and wine production.

In his interesting historical piece, Brian Johnston, a former CSIRO researcher and advisor and the co-author, with Janet Johnson, of the book *Wines of the Canberra District: Coming of Age*, describes the early efforts of various property owners who grew grapes in the Yass–Gunning area following the opening up of pastoral land for grazing in the early 1820s. The last of the original wineries in the region closed in 1908 and it was not until 1971 that the first of the commercial vineyards that now make up the Canberra District were established on the Murrumbateman and Lake George sites.

In the intervening 40 years, two varieties have emerged as particular strengths of the Canberra District: Riesling and Shiraz. In his article, Brian Croser, a doyen of the Australian wine industry and a speaker at the Third University House Symposium in 1979, first reflects on the history of the Canberra District, as well as that of the University House Wine Symposium itself, before turning his attention to Riesling—'the noblest white'. He charts the German origins of the variety and its history in Australia, he discusses the effect of climate and soil type on Riesling wine, and describes the combination of Riesling and Canberra as 'a compass point…in the biologically complex and variable world of fine wine'.

In his article, Dan Buckle, the winemaker at Mount Langi Ghiran, counters with the proclamation that '[i]n this country, Shiraz is king, at least so far', whilst noting in his historical overview of the variety that 'in France [Shiraz] has never had the noble, aristocratic status of Riesling, Chardonnay, Pinot Noir or Cabernet Sauvignon, and this indeed might be part of the reason this variety fits so well with Australia'. He highlights the large geographical expanse of Shiraz plantings in Australia, he draws a distinction between the falling prices for 'commodity' Shiraz-grape prices and the rising reputation (and price) of Australian Shiraz in the fine-wine market, and he rails against the recent tendency by some cool-climate winemakers to refer to the variety as 'Syrah'.

Although Shiraz and Riesling have emerged as the two pre-eminent varieties of the Canberra District, as Brian Johnston highlights in his article, many other varieties have been planted in the Canberra District, with a significant number of them gaining substantial recognition and success. As well as the expected mainstream varieties (Cabernet Sauvignon, Pinot Noir, Semillon, Sauvignon Blanc, and so on), recent years have seen the successful production in the Canberra District of wines from a range of other grape varieties, including Viognier, Sangiovese, Gruner Veltliner and Tempranillo. In the first of two articles on 'Emerging and Alternative Varieties', Libby Tassie, a viticultural consultant with a longstanding interest in alternative grape varieties, discusses the reasons for planting alternative varieties (potential climate change not least of these) and the challenges and choices involved. She emphasises the need for more comparative information and for more regional trials to determine the best fit for these new varieties. In his piece on the same topic, Nick Stock, one of Australia's most highly regarded and prolific wine commentators, recognises the importance of 'varietal exploration', but sounds a cautionary note. He warns (with characteristic forthrightness) against the trend of 'lesser producers in a region [failing] to make wine of sufficient quality in that region's most established/famous/successful/important/celebrated styles and so [taking] refuge in [the] obscurity [of alternative varieties] as a means of staying out of a competition they cannot win'. And he emphasises the importance of staying focused on producing *great* wine, not just different wine.

In the final paper of the proceedings, Brian Walsh, another of the most senior and most highly regarded figures of the Australian wine industry and currently the Director of Strategy and Business Development at Yalumba, considers the question 'is it better to have an average wine from an exceptional single site or an outstanding wine from a combination of sites'. He reflects on the concept of terroir, on the history of inter and intra-regional blending in Australia, and on the history—perhaps under-celebrated—of single-site wines in Australia. As he notes, 'many great fine [Australian] wines have been and will continue to be made' both from grapes from a combination of sites and from grapes from single vineyards. Both approaches are well represented in the wines now produced in the Canberra District and both have been rewarded with very considerable success.

References

Australian Academy of Science, 2010, 'The Science of Climate Change: Questions and Answers', http://www.science.org.au/policy/climatechange.html

Croser, B., 2011, '7th ANU University House Wine Symposium', May 22 2011, http://www.tapanappawines.com.au/blog/may2011/7th-anu-university-house-wine-symposium

Shanahan, C., 2011, 'Chilly climate at ANU Wine Symposium', Canberra Times, 15 June 2011, http://chrisshanahan.com/articles/2011/chilly-climate-at-anu-wine-symposium

8. Opening Speech

Professor Ian Young
Vice-Chancellor, ANU

I have great pleasure in welcoming you to The Australian National University, and to University House. In doing so, I would like to 'acknowledge the First Australians on whose land we meet and whose cultures we celebrate, as among the oldest continuing cultures in human history'.

University House is a very special part of the ANU. It was the first building completed and occupied on campus, having been designed as a residence for the research students and professors of the University, much along the lines of an Oxford or Cambridge college. It now has a much broader function, including as a venue where the University celebrates. It has hosted many significant events in the life of the University; Nelson Mandela dined here when he received an honorary degree from the University and Prince Frederick and Princess Mary of Denmark had their first official Australian engagement here in the Hall, where tomorrow night's gala dinner is to be held.

Even before the House opened in 1954, a wine committee had been formed, and the first Master, Professor Dale Trendall, ran the First University House Wine Symposium in 1956! John Lovering, who is here with us today, was a member of the committee for that important event when he was in the Research School of Earth Sciences. Richard Barwick, who is also here, was on the organising committees for several of our symposia. Importantly, he chose as the logo for the Third Symposium an image of the Greek cup kept in the House; that logo was adopted by the third Master, Professor Ralph Elliott, also with us, as the symbol for, and which is synonymous with, the House. Dr Barwick also designed the logo for this symposium.

Social historian Jill Waterhouse wrote the *Jubilee History of University House* in 2004, on the occasion of its fiftieth anniversary. In its opening chapters, she paints the interplay of the development of Canberra, the ANU and the House. The House has always been an institution in and of Canberra. It is fitting, therefore, in this year in which we recognise the fortieth anniversary of the plantings of vines that were the vanguard of the reborn wine industry in the Canberra District, that the House has focused this Seventh Wine Symposium on the Canberra and district wineries and wines—now widely recognised and highly regarded nationally.

The organisers have planned an integrated program of lectures, tastings, tours and a gala dinner, to highlight the district's best. Those who will be speaking to you today are leaders in the fields of viticulture, oenology, climate change and related areas. We are especially pleased to have with us for the whole symposium James Halliday, the foremost wine writer and critic in Australia. Mr Halliday is the guest speaker at dinner tomorrow night.

The ANU prides itself on excellence. Whether it be in philosophy, mathematics, Asian studies, public policy or many other academic endeavours, the University is a national leader and among a handful of leading universities in these fields internationally. Recognising the extraordinary quality of the district's wines, it pleases me greatly that the ANU can lead the fortieth anniversary celebrations of an industry not well recognised two decades ago but which has now come of age. Its transition to maturity is wonderfully captured in Brian Johnston and Janet Johnson's book, which is to be launched by the ACT Minister for Tourism in about 45 minutes, and of which you have been given a copy as part of your registration for the symposium.

It is my role formally to open the symposium. I have great delight in doing so and in wishing you well in your deliberations over the next two days. I will join you for dinner tomorrow night and look forward to the opportunity of meeting some of you and, as a recently arrived Canberra resident, discovering some of the best wines that the district has to offer.

Thank you.

9. Projected Climate: Means and extremes. How will this impact the wine industry?

Leanne Webb
University of Melbourne, Institute of Land and Food Resources
and CSIRO Marine and Atmospheric Research

Abstract

Changes to climate resulting from increasing concentrations of greenhouse gasses in the atmosphere are projected. For Australia, these projections indicate a warming climate with more warming in the central part of the continent and less in the coastal regions. For the Canberra region, the median annual warming projection (23 climate models) is in the order 0.9°C by 2030 compared with the 1990 baseline period. The direction of change in projections for rainfall is less certain for Australia with some models indicating a drier future climate, while others indicate a wetter future. For the Canberra region, the median projected annual rainfall (23 models) by 2030 is 2.2 per cent drier with a range from 7.8 per cent drier to 3.2 per cent wetter. Along with changes to mean temperature, projections for changes to extreme climate events have been quantified. Increases in extreme heat, extreme rainfall and intensity and frequency of droughts and bushfires have been described for the Australian continent.

These projected changes to climate will impact wine-grape growing in Australia. Some regions will be exposed to potentially greater impacts due to the spatially diverse nature of the changing climate. Changes to phenological phases and wine-grape quality are described. The vulnerability of viticulture to extreme events, both observed and projected, is also discussed.

Projected Climate Changes

Mean Climate

Australia and the globe are experiencing rapid climate change (IPCC 2007). Since the middle of the twentieth century, Australian temperatures have, on average, risen by about 1°C with an increase in the frequency of hot days and a decrease in the numbers of frosts and cold days. Rainfall patterns have also changed, but they are not uniform spatially; the north-west shows an increase in rainfall over the past 50 years while much of eastern Australia and the far south-west have experienced a decline (Australian Bureau of Meteorology 2011).

Further climate change is expected over the coming decades due to greenhouse gases emitted in the past that remain in the atmosphere and anticipated emissions in the future (IPCC 2007). As seen in Figure 1a, for most locations the projected best estimate[1] of mean warming over Australia by 2030 (mid emissions) is 0.7–0.9°C in coastal areas and 1–1.2°C in the inland regions. In winter, warming is projected to be a little less than in the other seasons—as low as 0.5°C in the far south by 2030. Warming is usually less near the coast than further inland, an exception being in the north-west, where the warming exceeds 1.3°C in spring (CSIRO and Australian Bureau of Meteorology 2007).

For 2030, the best estimates (fiftieth percentile) of precipitation change relative to 1990 for each season are shown in Figure 1b. Best estimates of annual precipitation change represent little change in the far north and decreases of 2 per cent to 5 per cent elsewhere. In summer and autumn, decreases are smaller and there are slight increases in the east. Decreases of about 5 per cent occur in winter and spring, particularly in the south-west where they reach 10 per cent (CSIRO and Australian Bureau of Meteorology 2007).

As well as the projected decline in rainfall, potential evapotranspiration (PEt) will increase as a function of projected increased temperature in all seasons and in all regions (CSIRO and Australian Bureau of Meteorology 2007).

Extreme Events

Increases in heatwave occurrences in eastern Australia and South Australia since the 1950s have been reported by Deo et al. (2007) and projected increases in their frequencies in future reported by Alexander and Arblaster (2009). Furthermore, an increased area is likely to be affected by drought with a reduction in recurrence interval (Hennessy et al. 2008). An increased risk of bushfires has also been modelled for south-eastern Australia (Lucas et al. 2007).

As well as changes to daily precipitation, the intensity of precipitation is likely to increase under enhanced greenhouse conditions (CSIRO and Australian Bureau of Meteorology 2007). There is also a projected increase in the number of dry days for Australia. Furthermore, for much of Australia there is an increased chance of extreme rainfall, though this varies seasonally (CSIRO and Australian Bureau of Meteorology 2007).

---

1 Median result (fiftieth percentile) from assessment of 23 climate models (CSIRO and Australian Bureau of Meteorology 2007).

9. Projected Climate: Means and extremes. How will this impact the wine industry?

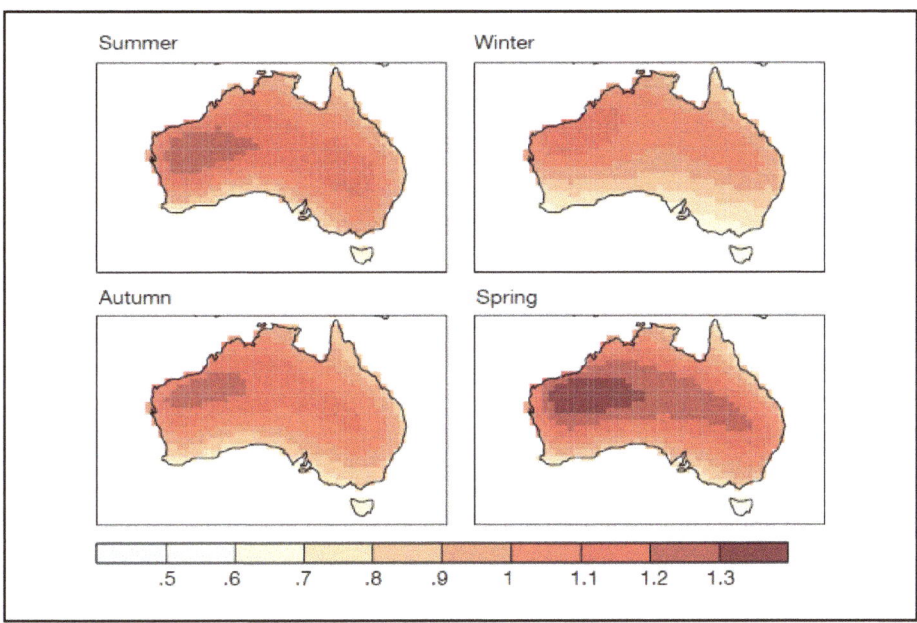

Figure 1a Best estimate (fiftieth percentile) of the seasonal change in average temperature (°C) over land by 2030 for the IPCC A1B emission scenario.

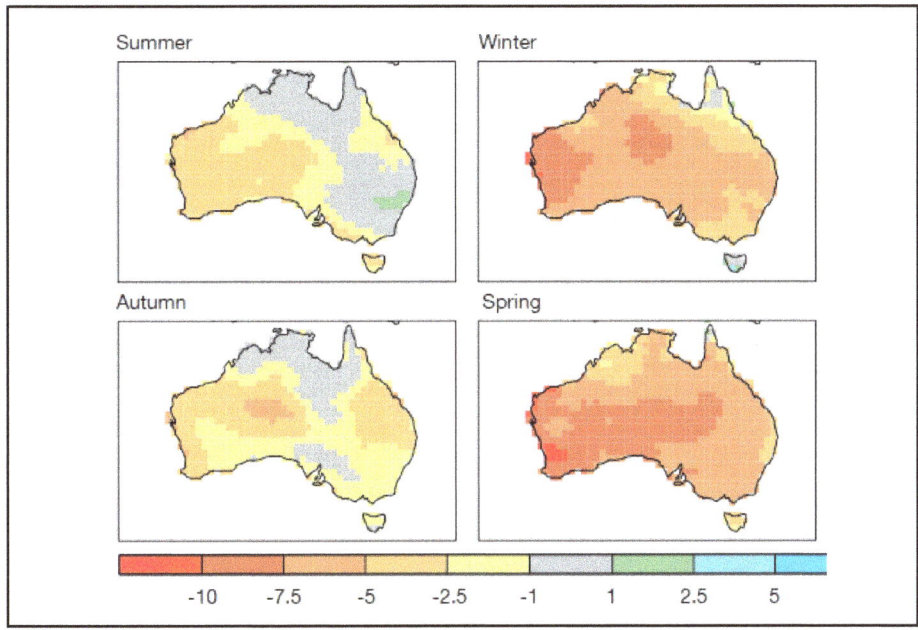

Figure 1b Best estimate (fiftieth percentile) of the projected seasonal change of precipitation by 2030 for the IPCC A1B emission scenario, as a percentage of 1961–90 values.

Proceedings of the 7th University House Wine Symposium

Climate Projections for the Canberra Winegrowing Region

Climate change projections are summarised for the Canberra Geographic Indication winegrowing region (Figure 2 and Table 1). The methodology and results presented here are consistent with those presented in the *Climate change in Australia* report (CSIRO and Australian Bureau of Meteorology 2007) whereby output from 23 models is used to determine the range of results. The model median is interpreted here as the best estimate for projected change and the model range describes the tenth and ninetieth percentiles of the distribution of model results. Projections for the year 2030 given a mid-estimate of greenhouse gas emissions (A1B) are presented alongside projections to 2070 calculated using a high greenhouse gas emission scenario (A1FI). See IPCC (2000) for a discussion of estimated greenhouse gas emissions into the future.

Figure 2 Canberra winegrowing region (pink) situated in the southern NSW winegrowing zone in Australia.

For Canberra, models suggest an increase of annual average temperatures of 0.9°C by 2030 compared with the 1990 baseline period, while annual rainfall is likely to decline (2.2 per cent). For this region, most of the warming occurs in summer and spring, with projected spring rainfall most likely to be affected by enhanced greenhouse conditions (Table 1). By 2070, the projected increase in annual average temperature is 3°C (2.1–4.2°C) and annual rainfall reductions of 7 per cent (25 per cent decrease to 10.4 per cent increase). These projections represent changes in climatic conditions averaged over several decades centred on 2030 and 2070.[2]

Table 1 Projected Climate Changes (Relative to 1990) for the Canberra Geographic Indication.

Canberra		Average of 2030 mid change (% or °C)		Average of 2070 high change (% or °C)	
Climate variable	Period	Model median	Model range	Model median	Model range
Temperature (°C)	Annual	0.9	0.6 to 1.3	3.0	2.1 to 4.2
	Summer	1.0	0.6 to 1.5	3.2	2.1 to 4.7
	Autumn	0.9	0.6 to 1.3	2.9	1.9 to 4.3
	Winter	0.8	0.5 to 1.1	2.5	1.7 to 3.6
	Spring	1.0	0.7 to 1.4	3.3	2.2 to 4.7
T_max (°C)	Annual	1.0	0.7 to 1.3	3.1	2.1 to 4.3
T_min (−C)	Annual	0.9	0.6 to 1.2	2.8	2.0 to 3.9
Rainfall (%)	Annual	−2.2	−7.8 to 3.2	−7.0	−25.1 to 10.4
	Summer	1.0	−7.0 to 10.3	3.2	−22.7 to 33.2
	Autumn	−0.9	−8.9 to 8.0	−3.0	−28.7 to 25.9
	Winter	−4.7	−12.2 to 3.5	−15.1	−39.4 to 11.4
	Spring	−5.5	−14.6 to 3.0	−17.9	−47.1 to 9.8

Note: Results are indicative in that they are based on the results of global climate models and do not take into account local topographical effects.

Of interest to wine-grape growers is the diurnal range (a measure of the difference in the minimum temperature and the maximum temperature recorded in a 24-hour period). To calculate this, projected change to maximum temperature (average temperature change multiplied by the ratio of change in maximum to mean temperature) and projected change to minimum temperature (average temperature change multiplied by the ratio of change in minimum to mean temperature) is first derived (CSIRO and Australian Bureau of Meteorology 2007). As changes to maximum temperatures are greater than changes to minimum temperatures in this region, the projected diurnal range is projected to increase (Table 1).

---

2 It is advisable to note that conditions of any individual year will be strongly affected by inter-annual and inter-decadal natural climatic variability and cannot be easily predicted.

Impacts for the Wine Industry

Phenology

Evidence suggests that as climate warms, wine-grape phenology (annual phases of growth) progresses more swiftly and grapes ripen earlier (Chuine et al. 2004; Jones et al. 2005). Over recent decades a trend to earlier maturity of wine grapes has been detected in 43 of 44 vineyard blocks studied across southern Australia (Webb et al. 2011). For the period 1993–2009, 35 of the 44 vineyard blocks indicated a statistically significant trend to earlier maturity. In all cases where earlier maturity was observed the region had undergone a warming trend.

Modelled impact of a future warming climate indicates that for most regions in Australia budburst and harvest will occur in an earlier part of the year (Webb et al. 2007) (Table 2). Furthermore, with future projected warming, grapevines will be ripening both in a warmer climate and at an earlier, hence warmer, part of the season (Webb et al. 2007) (Figure 3). At very cool sites, higher temperatures can be advantageous and wine-grape ripening can become more consistent (Ashenfelter and Storchmann 2010). Nevertheless, in most wine-grape growing regions in Australia, consequences of earlier ripening are undesirable.

Table 2 Impact on Phenology: Impacts of climate change on Cabernet Sauvignon budburst and harvest days (days cf. 1990) for two outlook periods, growing in Coonawarra and Riverland.

Phase	Region	2030	2050
Budburst	Coonawarra	3 to 7 days earlier	5 to 12 days earlier
	Riverland	2 to 4 days earlier	2 to 7 days earlier
Harvest	Coonawarra	15 to 23 days earlier	21 to 45 days earlier
	Riverland	6 to 13 days earlier	8 to 24 days earlier

Note: Each impact is presented as a range (in days) resulting from calculations using three climate models (CSIRO Mk3.0, DARLAM 125km and HADCM3) and three emission scenarios (A1FI, A1B, B1) (IPCC 2000).

Quality

Temperature at, and leading up to, harvest influences wine-grape quality (Coombe and Iland 2004; Jackson and Lombard 1993). Higher temperatures can reduce anthocyanin levels (Cozzolino et al. 2010; Haselgrove et al. 2000) and increase volatilisation of aroma compounds (Marais et al. 2001). A possible decoupling of sugar development from that of flavour and aroma components could have resulted in increased alcohol in wine in recent warmer vintages (Duchene and Schneider 2005; Godden and Gishen 2005). Levels of acids have also been shown to be temperature dependent. Liu et al. (2006) found that organic acids are sensitive to climate change and this sensitivity is greater for malic acid than for tartaric acid.

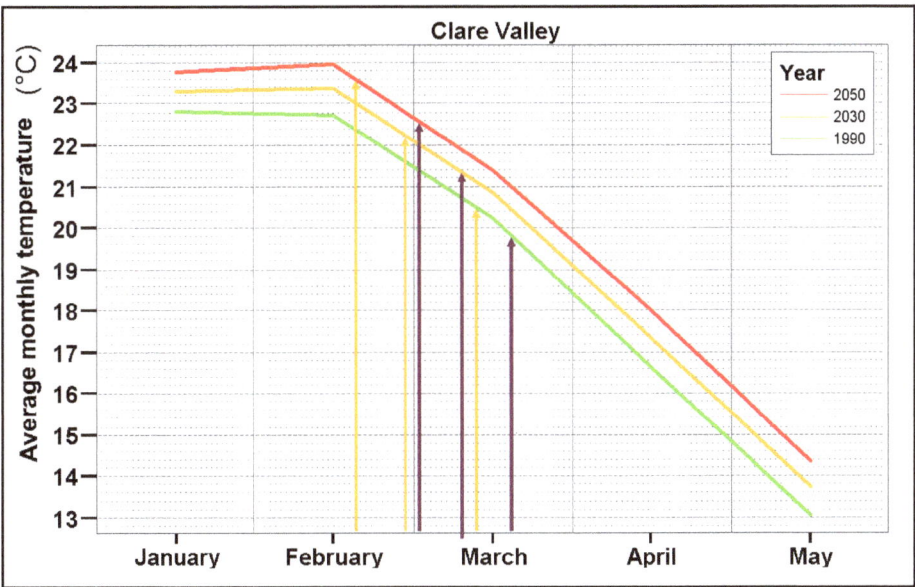

Figure 3 Projected Harvest Dates and Temperatures (°C) for the Clare Valley for the Baseline Year 1990 (green line), and Years 2030 (gold line) and 2050 (red line) for the A1B GHG Emission Scenario (mid emissions) and the CSIRO Mk 3.0 Climate Model.

Note: The yellow arrows indicate modelled Chardonnay harvest dates and the purple arrows indicate the Cabernet Sauvignon harvest dates for the relevant years (arrows touching the temperature curve).

As mentioned earlier, inland regions are projected to warm at a faster rate than coastal regions. Due to these non-uniform warming projections as well as the large spatial variation in climate where wine grapes are currently grown (Smart et al. 1980), the magnitude of impact of future climate change on wine quality varies across Australia (Webb et al. 2008). Where targeted adaptation practices are implemented, some existing cooler regions could benefit from a warming climate.

Reduced Water

Most of Australia's vineyards are irrigated and rely on a secure irrigation supply (McCarthy et al. 1992); therefore, the impact of climate change is likely to be perceived through reduced water availability resulting from decreased rainfall in catchments supplying irrigation. Lower rainfalls are associated with proportionally larger reductions in stream flow that will substantially reduce available water in public storages, rivers and on-farm dams (Cai and Cowan 2008; Cai et al. 2009; Potter et al. 2008).

Extreme Events

An increasing frequency of extreme temperature events has the potential to affect crops more than higher temperatures per se. For example, a 15-day 'hot spell' (above 35°C) in South Australia during the harvest period in March 2008 (Australian Bureau of Meteorology 2008) resulted in large quality reductions and fermentation problems (Hook 2008). Furthermore, many ripe grapes were unable to be processed by wineries that were already at full capacity (AWBC 2008).

The exceptional heatwave that occurred in south-eastern Australia during late January and early February 2009 also resulted in unprecedented impacts. At this time, most of the south-eastern Australian wine-grape crop was in the veraison (berry softening and commencement of sugar accumulation) or post-veraison stage of its phenology (McIntyre et al. 1982). Significant heat-stress–related crop losses were also reported at many sites (Webb et al. 2010).

In changing global climatic conditions the risk of frost incidence is likely to change. Future temperature projections indicate fewer frost days so it might be expected that horticulturists would experience less frost damage. As the timing of budburst for perennial crops controlled by temperature and budburst is likely to occur earlier in the year, frost risk might not be reduced (Hanninen 1991; Nemani et al. 2001). In some regions, projections of lower rainfall in spring and associated drier soils, fewer clouds and lower dew points (CSIRO and Australian Bureau of Meteorology 2007) might even increase frost risk (Snyder and Paulo de Melo-Abreu 2005). Furthermore, an increase in day-to-day climate variability could lessen any 'positive' impact of mean warming on reducing frost frequency (Rigby and Porporato 2008).

With the incidence of bushfires projected to increase (Lucas et al. 2007), the risk of smoke taint is likely to increase. Smoke from bushfires and controlled burning can reduce the sensory characteristics of wine, leading to 'smoke taint' (Kennison et al. 2009) and an unsaleable product. Wine is adversely affected by the smoke-taint–related compounds (guaiacol and 4-methylguaiacol) that are released throughout the fermentation process. Smoke taint due to wildfires cost Australian grape growers more than $7.5 million during the 2003 and 2004 vintages (Whiting and Krstic 2007).

Although average rainfall is projected to decrease, the frequency of extreme rainfall events is likely to increase by up to 4 per cent in south-eastern Australia during the harvest period in autumn (CSIRO and Australian Bureau of Meteorology 2007). Consequences of increased frequency of extreme rainfall events include flood damage, erosion damage and increased disease pressure after such events. Along with the risk of berry splitting and berry drop due to abscission, *Botrytis cinerea* (grey mould) develops in wet and humid conditions and can devastate wine-grape crops close to and during harvest. Therefore, any heavy rainfall at this time represents a serious risk (Magarey et al. 1994).

The Canberra District and much of south-eastern Australia experienced very wet conditions in October 2010 and February 2011 associated with the 2010 La Niña event and also very high sea-surface temperatures at this time (Australian Bureau of Meteorology 2010) (Figure 4). During these periods many vineyards were exposed to very much above average rainfall. These events led to increased incidences of disease in vineyards across south-eastern Australia, as well as inundation of some lower-lying vineyards. Other impacts reported were more difficulty in accessing fungicides at this time and also transport and logistics being impacted.

Conclusion

Changes to climate resulting from increasing concentrations of greenhouse gasses in the atmosphere are projected. For Australia, these projections indicate a warming climate with more warming in the central part of the continent and less in the coastal regions. The direction of change in projections for rainfall are less certain for Australia, with some models indicating a drier future climate, while others indicate a wetter future. Along with changes to mean temperature, projections for changes to extreme climate events have been quantified. Increases in extreme heat, extreme rainfall and intensity and frequency of droughts and bushfires have been described for the Australian continent.

For the Canberra region, the median annual warming projection (23 climate models) is in the order 0.9°C by 2030 compared with the 1990 baseline period. Phenological phases are likely to be earlier in a warming climate and this has implications for wine-grape quality.

For the Canberra region, the median projected annual rainfall (23 models) by 2030 is 2.2 per cent drier with a range from 7.8 per cent drier to 3.2 per cent wetter. Water requirements for grapevines are likely to increase while at the same time rainfall and associated runoff to water storages are likely to decrease. Water-use efficiency measures are therefore likely to become more important in future.

Changes in mean temperatures will be gradual, giving wine industry practitioners time to adapt. Extreme events—heatwaves, bushfires, extreme rainfall and drought—are all projected to increase in frequency and severity in future and these are what could have the greatest impact on wine-grape enterprises, at least in the shorter term.

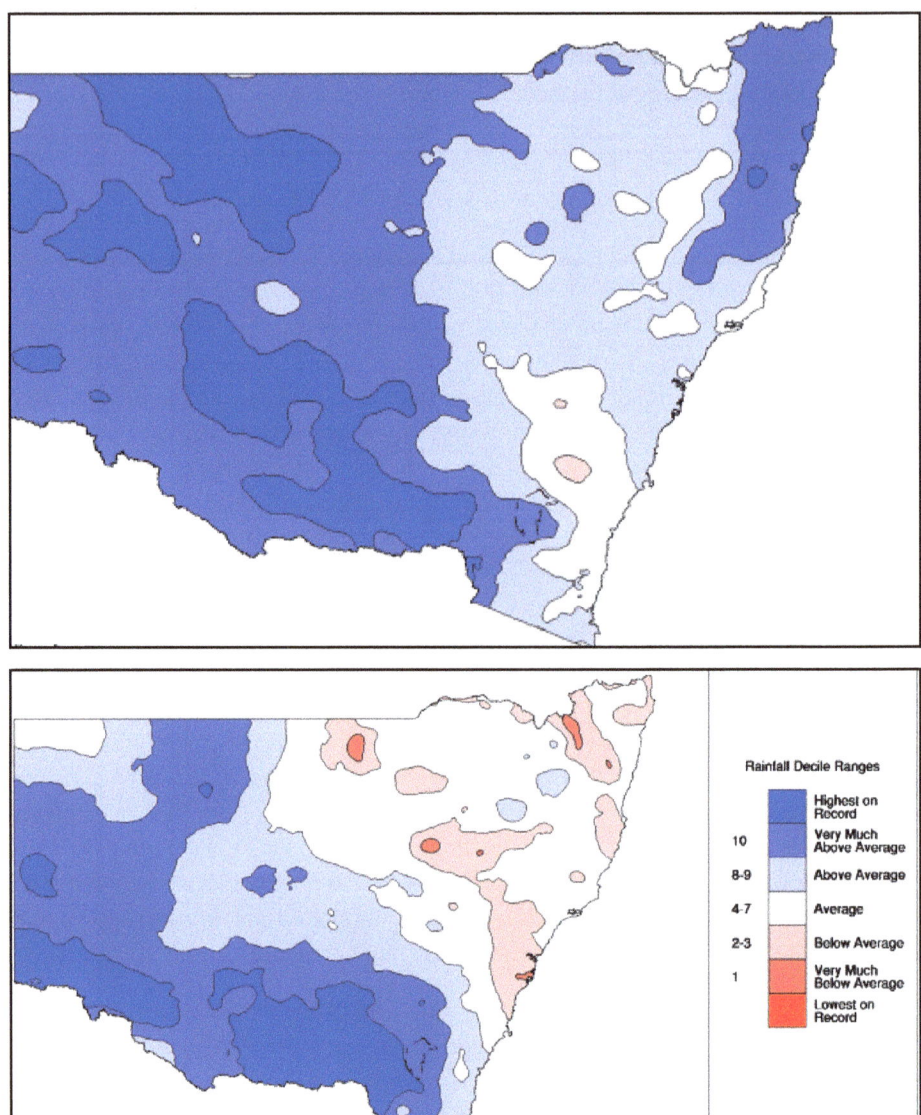

Figure 4 NSW Rainfall Deciles for October 2010 (top) and February 2011 (bottom).

Source: Bureau of Meteorology, <http://www.bom.gov.au/jsp/awap/rain/index.jsp>

References

Alexander, L. V. and Arblaster, J. M., 2009, 'Assessing trends in observed and modelled climate extremes over Australia in relation to future projections', *International Journal of Climatology*, vol. 29, pp. 417–35, <http://dx.doi.org/10.1002/joc.1730>

Ashenfelter, O. C. and Storchmann, K., 2010, 'Measuring the economic effect of global warming on viticulture using auction, retail, and wholesale prices', *Review of Industrial Organization*, vol. 37, pp. 51–64.

Australian Bureau of Meteorology, 2008, *Long-term rainfall deficiencies continue in southern Australia while wet conditions dominate the north*, Special Climate Statement 16, 10 October 2008, Bureau of Meteorology, Canberra, viewed 1 May 2009, <http://www.bom.gov.au/climate/current/statements/scs16.pdf>

Australian Bureau of Meteorology, 2010, *Annual Climate Summary*, Bureau of Meteorology, Canberra, <http://www.bom.gov.au/climate/annual_sum/2010/AnClimSum10_LR1.0.pdf>

Australian Bureau of Meteorology, 2011, *Fact Sheet 2*, Bureau of Meteorology, Canberra, <http://www.bom.gov.au/climate/change/docs/FactSheet3.pdf>

Australian Wine and Brandy Corporation (AWBC), 2008, Web site, viewed 13 November 2007, <http://www.wineaustralia.com/Australia/Default.aspx?tabid=302>

Cai, W. and Cowan, T., 2008, 'Evidence of impacts from rising temperature on inflows to the Murray–Darling Basin', *Geophysical Research Letters*, vol. 35, no. L07701.

Cai, W., Cowan, T., Briggs, P. R. and Raupach, M. R., 2009, 'Rising temperature depletes soil moisture and exacerbates severe drought conditions across southeast Australia', *Geophysical Research Letters*, vol. 36, no. L21709.

Chuine, I., Yiou, P., Viovy, N., Seguin, B., Daux, V. and Ladurie, E. L. R., 2004, 'Historical phenology: grape ripening as a past climate indicator', *Nature*, vol. 432, pp. 289–90, <http://www.nature.com/nature/journal/v432/n7015/suppinfo/432289a_S1.html>

Coombe, B. G. and Iland, P., 2004, 'Grape berry development and winegrape quality', in P. R. Dry and B. G. Coombe (eds), *Viticulture. Volume 1: Resources*, [Second edition], Winetitles, Adelaide, pp. 210–48.

Cozzolino, D., Cynkar, W. U., Dambergs, R. G., Gishen, M. and Smith, P., 2010, 'Grape (*Vitis vinifera*) compositional data spanning ten successive vintages in the context of abiotic growing parameters', *Agriculture, Ecosystems & Environment*, vol. 139, p. 565, <http://www.sciencedirect.com/science/article/B6T3Y-5196KH0-2/2/4f33cc3c6504d1c79494d9e2be10f70e>

CSIRO and Australian Bureau of Meteorology, 2007, *Climate change in Australia*, Technical report, CSIRO and Bureau of Meteorology through the Australian Climate Change Science Program, Melbourne, <http://climatechangeinaustralia.com.au/technical_report.php>

Deo, R. C., McAlpine, C. A., Syktus, J., McGowan, H. A. and Phinn, S., 2007, 'On Australian heat waves: time series analysis of extreme temperature events in Australia, 1950–2005', in L. Oxley and D. Kulasiri (eds), *MODSIM 2007 International Congress on Modelling and Simulation*, Modelling and Simulation Society of Australia and New Zealand, pp. 626–35.

Duchene, E. and Schneider, C., 2005, 'Grapevine and climatic changes: a glance at the situation in Alsace', *Agronomy for Sustainable Development*, vol. 24, pp. 93–9.

Godden, P. and Gishen, M., 2005, 'Trends in the composition of Australian wine', *Australian and New Zealand Wine Industry Journal*, vol. 20, pp. 21–46.

Hanninen, H., 1991, 'Does climatic warming increase the risk of frost damage in northern trees', *Plant Cell And Environment*, vol. 14, pp. 449–54.

Haselgrove, L., Botting, D., Van Heeswijck, R., Hoj, P. B., Dry, P. R., Ford, C. and Iland, P. G., 2000, 'Canopy microclimate and berry composition: the effect of bunch exposure on the phenolic composition of *Vitis vinifera* L cv. Shiraz grape berries', *Australian Journal of Grape and Wine Research*, vol. 6, pp. 141–9.

Hennessy, K., Fawcett, R., Kirono, D., et al., 2008, *An Assessment of the Impact of Climate Change on the Nature and Frequency of Exceptional Climatic Events*, CSIRO and Bureau of Meteorology, Melbourne, <http://www.daff.gov.au/__data/assets/pdf_file/0007/721285/csiro-bom-report-future-droughts.pdf>

Hook, J., 2008, 'Heatwave effects on South Australian vineyards—observations in 2008', *Australian and New Zealand Grapegrower and Winemaker*, vol. 533, pp. 25–6.

Intergovernmental Panel on Climate Change (IPCC), 2000, *Special Report on Emission Scenarios—A special report of Working Group III of the Intergovernmental Panel on Climate Change*, Cambridge University Press, Cambridge, <http://www.grida.no/climate/ipcc/emission/index.htm>

Intergovernmental Panel on Climate Change (IPCC), 2007, *Climate Change 2007: The physical science basis. Contribution of Working Group I to the Fourth Assessment Report of the Intergovernmental Panel on Climate Change*, Cambridge University Press, Cambridge, <http://www.ipcc.ch/pdf/assessment-report/ar4/syr/ar4_syr_spm.pdf>

Jackson, D. I. and Lombard, P. B., 1993, 'Environmental and management practices affecting grape composition and wine quality—a review', *American Journal for Enology and Viticulture*, vol. 44, pp. 409–30.

Jones, G. V., Duchene, E., Tomasi, D., et al., 2005, 'Changes in European winegrape phenology and relationships with climate', *Groupe d'Etude des Systemes de Conduite de la vigne (GESCO)*, pp. 54–61.

Kennison, K. R., Wilkinson, K. L., Pollnitz, A. P., Williams, H. G. and Gibberd, M. R., 2009, 'Effect of timing and duration of grapevine exposure to smoke on the composition and sensory properties of wine', *Australian Journal of Grape and Wine Research*, vol. 15, pp. 228–37, <http://dx.doi.org/10.1111/j.1755-0238.2009.00056.x>

Liu, H. F., Wu, B. H., Fan, P. G., Li, S. H. and Li, L. S., 2006, 'Sugar and acid concentrations in 98 grape cultivars analyzed by principal component analysis', *Journal of the Science of Food and Agriculture*, vol. 86, pp. 1526–36.

Lucas, C., Hennessy, K. J., Mills, G. A. and Bathols, J., 2007, *Bushfire weather in southeast Australia—recent trends and projected climate change impacts*, Consultancy report prepared by the Bushfire Cooperative Research Centre, Australian Bureau of Meteorology and CSIRO Marine and Atmospheric Research for the Climate Institute of Australia, Melbourne, viewed 22 July 2008, <http://www.cmar.csiro.au/e-print/open/2007/hennesseykj_c.pdf>

McCarthy, M. G., Jones, L. D. and Due, G., 1992, 'Irrigation—principles and practices', in B. G. Coombe and P. R. Dry (eds), *Viticulture. Volume 2: Practices*, Winetitles, Adelaide, pp. 104–28.

McIntyre, G. N., Lider, L. A. and Ferrari, N. L., 1982, 'The chronological classification of grapevine phenology', *American Journal for Enology and Viticulture*, vol. 33, pp. 80–5.

Magarey, P. A., Wachtel, M. F. and Nicholas, P. R., 1994, 'Diseases', in P. Nicholas, P. Magarey and M. Wachtel (eds), *Diseases and Pests. Grape Production Series. Number 1*, Winetitles, Adelaide, pp. 2–44.

Marais, J., Calitz, F. and Haasbroek, P. D., 2001, 'Relationship between microclimatic data, aroma component concentrations and wine quality parameters in the prediction of Sauvignon Blanc wine quality', *South African Journal for Enology and Viticulture*, vol. 22, pp. 22–6.

Nemani, R. R., White, M. A., Cayan, D. R., Jones, G. V., Running, S. W., Coughlan, J. C. and Peterson, D. L., 2001, 'Asymmetric warming over coastal California and its impact on the premium wine industry', *Climate Research*, vol. 19, pp. 25–34.

Potter, N. J., Chiew, F. H. S., Frost, A. J., Srikanthan, R., McMahon, T. A., Peel, M. C. and Austin, J. M., 2008, *Characterisation of recent rainfall and runoff in the Murray–Darling Basin*, A report to the Australian Government from the CSIRO Murray–Darling Basin Sustainable Yields Project: Water for a Healthy Country Flagship, viewed 22 April 2009, <http://www.csiro.au/files/files/pmax.pdf>

Rigby, J. R. and Porporato, A., 2008, 'Spring frost risk in a changing climate', *Geophysical Research Letters*, vol. 35, no. L12703.

Smart, R. E., Alcorso, C. and Hornsby, D. A., 1980, 'A comparison of winegrape performance at the present limits of Australian viticultural climates—Alice Springs and Hobart', *The Australian Grapegrower and Winemaker*, vol. 184, pp. 28 and 30.

Snyder, R. L. and Paulo de Melo-Abreu, J., 2005, *Frost Protection: Fundamentals, practice, and economics. Volume 1*, FAO Environment and Natural Resources Series 10, Food and Agriculture Organisation, Rome, <http://www.fao.org/docrep/008/y7223e/y7223e00.htm>

Webb, L., Whetton, P. and Barlow, E. W. R., 2007, 'Modelled impact of future climate change on phenology of wine grapes in Australia', *Australian Journal of Grape and Wine Research*, vol. 13, pp. 165–75.

Webb, L, Whetton, P. and Barlow, E. W. R., 2008, 'Climate change and wine grape quality in Australia', *Climate Research*, vol. 36, pp. 99–111.

Webb, L., Whiting, J., Watt, A. et al., 2010, 'Managing grapevines through severe heat: a survey of growers after the 2009 summer heatwave in south-eastern Australia', *Journal of Wine Research*, vol. 21, pp. 147–65, <http://www.informaworld.com/10.1080/09571264.2010.530106>

Webb, L. B., Whetton, P. H. and Barlow, E. W. R., 2011, 'Observed trends in winegrape maturity in Australia', *Global Change Biology*, vol. 17, pp. 2707–19, <http://dx.doi.org/10.1111/j.1365-2486.2011.02434.x>

Whiting, J. R. and Krstic, M., 2007, *Understanding the Sensitivity to Timing and Management Options to Mitigate the Negative Impacts of Bush Fire Smoke on Grape and Wine Quality—Scoping study*, Department of Primary Industries, Primary Industries Research, Knoxfield, Vic., <http://www.gwrdc.com.au/downloads/ResearchTopics/GWR%2006-03%20final%20report.pdf>

10. A Brief History of the Canberra District

Brian Johnston
McKellar Ridge Wines

Introduction

The history of the establishment of grape-growing and winemaking in what is now known as the Canberra District is a story in two parts. The first relates to pioneering efforts of various property owners who grew grapes in the Yass–Gunning area following the opening up of pastoral land for grazing in the area in the early 1820s. The second relates to the establishment of commercial vineyards in the area surrounding the Australian Capital Territory in the early 1970s and the establishment of the Canberra District as we now know it.

It is worth recalling the very early history of grape-growing in Australia. The first commercial vineyard in Australia was the Rose Hill vineyard established at Parramatta from cuttings brought to Australia by Governor Phillip on the First Fleet. In 1791 there were reported to be 3 acres (1.2 ha) of vines growing at Rose Hill. Grape-growing slowly spread as new settlers arrived, some with grape-growing experience. Captain John Macarthur established Camden Park in the early 1820s with more than 8 ha of vines, and that property subsequently played an important role in the importation and distribution of vine cuttings throughout New South Wales and the Barossa Valley.

Early Plantings in the Yass–Gunning Area

The first recorded planting of vines in the Yass–Gunning area was made by Dr Benjamin Clayton, who established a property called Baltinglass in the mid 1830s. He trained for medical practice in Sydney and travelled to London for his medical exams, completing a Certificate of Surgery with the Royal College in May 1828. Following his marriage to Fanny Broughton in 1835, he took up land at Baltinglass about 2 km outside Gunning where he also operated as the local doctor for nearly 20 years. By the mid 1840s, the property was highly regarded, having sheep, cattle and grapevines, as well as a substantive house. It is reported that he cultivated every variety of grape known and experimented in producing wine. He is reported to have produced an excellent Gunning wine that was awarded a medal in France, although details of this award have yet to be fully described. A watercolour of the property made in 1866 shows several acres of vines.

Dr Clayton was not the only Yass–Gunning grape-growing pioneer. Others included John Hardy, who planted grapes at Hardwicke near Yass, Hamilton Hume at Cooma Cottage, Robert Campbell, a Sydney merchant and large landowner who established a small vineyard at Duntroon in the 1860s, as well as a number of others.

Helm and Cambourne (1999) report that records from the Colonial Secretary's Office show that by 1858 there were 5 ha of vines planted to wine grapes in the County of King (including Yass), producing 1660 gallons (7550 L) of wine and 230 gallons (1000 L) of brandy. However, Helm and Cambourne reported that wine production in the district by 1908 had become uneconomic, with the last winery, Ainsbury near Yass, closing its doors in that year. This was due to a combination factors including the activities of the Temperance Movement reducing consumption, the depression of 1893 and the flood of wine from South Australia and Victoria that followed Federation in 1901.

The Resurgence of the Canberra District

A resurgence of interest in grape-growing in the district occurred with the establishment of Canberra as the nation's capital and the influx of new families. The first known vineyard in the ACT was established by the Forner family, when Clem Forner moved from Griffith in 1925 to work in the ACT and took up an orchard lease at Narrabundah. (Interestingly, Clem was a friend of the De Bortoli family who established the wine empire at Griffith.) The vineyard at Narrabundah comprised about 1.2 ha and grew both red and white grapes, the family making what were described as 'Chablis' and 'Cabernet' style wines. It was only when the ACT Government began resuming leases for housing in the late 1950s that the vineyard was removed.

The Scientific Pioneers

By the mid 1960s, Canberra was a thriving city with many fine academic institutions, including The Australian National University, the John Curtin School of Medical Research and the CSIRO. It is from these institutions that the rebirth of the Canberra District, as we now know it, was to come.

Four names initially stand out: Dr Edgar Riek and Ken Helm, both from CSIRO Division of Entomology, Dr John Kirk from the CSIRO Division of Plant Industry and the lesser known Dr Max Blake from the John Curtin School of Medical

Research. Evidence gathered during the preparation of our book *Wines of the Canberra District: Coming of age* (2011) has revealed an interesting time line of early plantings and subsequent commercial production.

Dr Riek, who has a passion for fine wines and fine food, was the first Cellar Master for the Canberra Food and Wine Club in 1953. He also knew a number of Rutherglen and Milawa winemakers well, including Mick Morris and the Brown brothers, becoming involved in Muscat maturation trials and wine judging at the Rutherglen Wine Show in the early 1960s. He decided Canberra had the climate for growing grapes and thought he would put his skills to the test. He acquired a set of grape cuttings from the CSIRO Merbein Research Station in 1966 and planted them in his garden in Ainslie. In 1967 these were planted out on a friend's property at Sutton. When he returned from overseas at the end of 1968, he was disappointed to find the cuttings were doing poorly due to the harsh summer conditions. This led to the search for a better site.

Luckily, his wife had spotted a number of blocks for sale on the edge of Lake George, about 50 km north of Canberra. Edgar was familiar with the microclimate of the area, having driven past the site in the middle of winter over the years. He had noticed the 'warmer' conditions on the edge of Lake George, as the car windows defrosted when he drove by.

In November 1970 the 'Cullarin' site was purchased and it has proved to be warmer than Canberra by an average of 2°C during winter. With good drainage and a natural spring, Cullarin proved to be an excellent grape-growing site.

Dr Riek planted the first half-acre of grapes in 1971, using a rotary hoe to prepare the site and planting vegetables—sweet corn, tomatoes and beans—between the rows to assist with family self-sufficiency. A 100-year-old slab hut was renovated to provide shelter during vintage, and plantings gradually expanded. The early grapes were planted without the benefit of drip irrigation and usually took four years before they bore significant fruit.

Also in 1968, while Dr Riek was facing the disappointment of the poor establishment of his cuttings at Sutton, Dr Max Blake was having more success on his property near Bungendore, where a trial plot of 100 vines was successfully established (Helm and Cambourne 1999). This site was subsequently abandoned and he went on to establish a 4 ha vineyard at nearby Brooks Creek in 1973, which he named Shingle House.

The year 1971 has also proven to be a significant year in the re-establishment of the Canberra District for a second reason: Dr Kirk and his family planted the first vines at Clonakilla, a property on the outskirts of Murrumbateman. One hectare of vines was planted in 1971—Cabernet Sauvignon and Riesling.

Dr Kirk initially planted the vines on a relatively low area of the property and they grew well in the first year, which was relatively wet. This encouraged him to expand his plantings to 1.5 ha the following season. The summer of 1972–73 was a shock—a drought had arrived—and, without irrigation, many of the vines were severely water stressed and many died. Some of the first plantings, which were at the bottom of the hill, received some moisture from the ground and survived, but most of the new, second-year plantings and the first died, leaving about 0.5 ha under vines. The dry, hot summers also encouraged the brown grasshoppers to feed on the young vines, causing further damage, along with that from rabbits and cockatoos. Despite these setbacks and with the advent of drip irrigation, by 1978, the vineyard was eventually well established further up the slopes of the property.

In 1973 five more growers began to establish vineyards in the district (Table 1).

Table 1 Development of the First Canberra District Vineyards, 1971–86.

Vineyard	Developer	Year grapes were first planted
Cullarin Cellars (later renamed Lake George Wines)	Dr Edgar Riek	1971
Clonakilla	Dr John Kirk	1971
Nanima Creek Vineyard (now known as Helm Wines)	Ken Helm	1973
Doonkuna Estate	Wing Commander Harvey Smith	1973
Broughton Park (now known as Murrumbateman Wines)	Geoff and Trish Middleton	1973
Westering Vineyard (now Lake George Wines)	Captain Geoff Hood	1973
Shingle House (later known as Brooks Creek)	Dr Max Blake	1973
Affleck Vineyard	Dr Ian and Susie Hendry	1976
Telofa (now known as Yass Valley Wines)	Peter Griffith	1978
Lark Hill	Dr Dave and Sue Carpenter	1978
Benfield Estate (near Yass, no longer operational)	David and Lanette Fetherston	1979
Appletree Hill Vineyard, Queanbeyan (no longer exists)	Dr David Madew, sr	1980
Jeir Creek	Rob and Kay Howell	1984
Ruker Wines (now Linberi Park)	Rick Ruker	1984
Mamre (now Kyeema Vineyard)	Ron McKenzie	1985
Brindabella Hills	Dr Roger and Faye Harris	1986
Pankhurst	Allan and Christine Pankhurst	1986
Park Lane (now Surveyors Hill)	Alwyn Lane	1986

Source: Helm (1979); Helm and Cambourne (1999); author's own research.

In 1973, Ken Helm, who went on to be a particularly outstanding producer of Riesling wine in the district, planted his first vines at his Nanima Creek vineyard—the same year as Wing Commander Harvey Smith planted Doonkuna, Geoff and Trish Middleton planted Broughton Park, Captain Geoff Hood planted Westering Vineyard and, as noted, Dr Max Blake planted Shingle House.

One of the features of the establishment of the Canberra District in the post-1971 era has been the willingness to learn and share with each other. The inaugural meeting of the Canberra District Winegrowers' Association, attended by seven people, was held at Dr Riek's home in November 1974. It was decided to form the association to further exchange information and experiences on grape-growing and winemaking in the area and the association became active during 1975.

The Early Wines

Also in 1975 Dr Riek made his first wine, which included small volumes of red and white varieties. This was shared with friends and wine industry contacts, being bottled as 'Cullarin Cellars'. He visited France on a number of occasions, taking particular note of grape-growing and winemaking practices in Burgundy to see what he could apply at Cullarin.

The first wines sold commercially in the modern era were made by Dr John Kirk at the family's Clonakilla property in 1976. These first wines were a white wine blend of Riesling and Sauvignon Blanc and a red wine of Cabernet Sauvignon and Shiraz, both produced in small quantities. Dr Kirk sourced some fruit from Doonkuna to help make these wines.

Ken Helm made a Riesling in 1977 and in 1978 he combined with Geoff Middleton to make more small batches of wine. The 1977 Helm Riesling won First Prize in the 1977 Forbes Wine Show—the first wine show medal from the district in the modern era. The following year, also using additional fruit from Doonkuna, they combined to produce 3000 bottles of wine. A Riesling was subsequently offered for sale at the 1979 ANU Wine Symposium organised by the late Jim Murphy (of Murphy Cellars). It was attended by industry leaders including Wolf Blass and Max Schubert, the developer of Grange Hermitage. The Riesling was received with considerable enthusiasm by the delegates and utilised a special Canberra District Vignerons Association label.

The Helm Riesling went on to win further prizes in the 1978 and 1979 Forbes Wine shows, winning Champion Dry White in 1978 and First Prize in 1979. The 1978 Riesling also won First Prize in the Canberra National Show (Amateur Winemakers).

A number of the early Clonakilla wines were also entered in the Forbes Wine Show with considerable success. Also in 1978, three red wines received more than 17 points out of twenty. In 1979, the 1977 Cabernet Shiraz from Clonakilla was judged Best Red Wine of the Show and Clonakilla also won the port class.

At the same 1979 Forbes Show, the Helm–Middleton Chardonnay won Best Dry White, Dr Riek won the Rose and Sauterne classes and Helm–Middleton won Best 1979 Dry Red for their Cabernet Shiraz. These early successes gave great heart to the pioneering winemakers and, with greater awareness of potential and interest, a further 11 vineyards were planted between 1976 and 1986 (see Table 1).

Two of these early vineyards are now gone: Benefield Estate near Yass and Appletree Hill Vineyard in Queanbeyan, which was subsequently used for housing. Shingle House Vineyard (now known as Brooks Creek) is now being revitalised by the owners of Little Bridge Wines, after being effectively abandoned for a number of years.

Great Wines from Diverse Sites

As outlined in our chapter 'Award winning wines' in the new edition of the book *Wines of the Canberra District: Coming of age*, many wines from across diverse sites are now achieving the highest level of quality and success. The successful varietal range is expanding with Chardonnay, Tempranillo, Sangiovese, Cabernet, Merlot, Voignier, Semillon/Sauvignon Blanc, Pinot Gris and Gruner Veltliner all winning gold medals in recent years. The analysis indicates more than 200 gold and trophy medals have been awarded to Canberra District wines in the past five years—an average of more than 40 a year. In an interesting coincidence, it is also 40 years since Dr Riek and Dr Kirk planted their first commercial vines in 1971. On the basis of this evidence, it seems eminently fair to conclude that the district has truly 'come of age'.

References

Helm, K., 1979, 'Cool climate grape growing', in *Wine Talk*, Acton Press, Canberra.

Helm, K. and Cambourne, B., 1999, 'Canberra District: the cool climate wine capital', *Australian Wine Industry Journal*, vol. 16, no. 6.

Johnston, B. and Johnson, J., 2011, *Wines of the Canberra District: Coming of age*, 3R Operations, Canberra.

11. Riesling: The noblest white

Brian Croser

It's an honour to be invited to address the Seventh University House Wine Symposium especially as it is a celebration of 40 years of the modern Canberra wine industry. I have been witness to the emerging Canberra wine community for 34 of the 40 years being celebrated.

I love coming to Canberra and have had plenty of reasons over the past three decades to do so.

A little bit of personal local history is germane to my discussion of Riesling given the evident synergy between Canberra and Riesling.

My contact with the Canberra wine community has been continuous and frequent since the 1970s, as a judge and chairman at the Canberra National Wine Show, working with Edgar Riek and Bill Moore, as an industry politician, sparring about the appropriate tax for wine with John Dawkins, Peter Costello, Ken Helm, Richard Farmer and others for the decade of the 1990s and more recently as Chairman of the Canberra Regional Wine Show.

Two of my daughters have lived and worked for the Government here, one attended ANU and now lectures here on war. For 20 years my boffin brother has designed and made radars in his laboratory-factory next to the airport at Fyshwick and my fourth grandchild is due to be born in Canberra at the beginning of July. I feel like I know the place.

As inaugural lecturer in Wine Science at the then Riverina College of Advanced Education—now Charles Sturt University—in 1977 and 1978, I was in the district when Edgar Riek at Lake George, John Kirk at Clonakilla, Geoff Hood at Westerling, Ken Helm at Helm Wines and Sue and David Carpenter at Lark Hill and others were grappling with the challenges of being pioneer vignerons in the then unknown and frost-prone Canberra wine district.

The knowledge of how to match variety to environment in Australia was a largely ignored science in the 1970s. Most vineyards of the time were planted as 'fruit salad' vineyards to take advantage of the emerging market interest in grape varieties newly reintroduced to Australian vineyards. Chardonnay, Sauvignon Blanc, Gewürztraminer, Pinot Noir and Merlot and others were regarded as exotic varieties in a market just beginning to grow out of Hock, Chablis, White Burgundy, Claret and Burgundy and beginning to recognise varietal flavour differences. There was genuine excitement in the marketplace about the different and identifiable flavours of varietal wine and some memorable anomalous combinations were the Seppelt Bin Pinot Noirs from the Victorian Sunraysia district and Rutherglen and the many Gewürztraminers and Sauvignon Blancs from the Hunter. In 1979 Chardonnay was not yet ubiquitous; only 1471 tonnes were produced compared with 21 464 tonnes of Riesling (Australian Wine and Brandy Producers 1980).

The pioneer Canberra vineyards were also multi-varietal experiments with successes and failures in the unique and challenging Canberra terroir. Fortunately most of the new 'fruit salad' vineyards of the time also included the time-tested and true: (Rhine) Riesling, Shiraz and Cabernet Sauvignon. The first two of these have proven to be superior in their response to the unique Canberra terroir over the 40-year experiment that is the Canberra wine community.

In August 1979 I was privileged to be a speaker at the Third University House Symposium, addressing the issue of 'Australian white wines—their history, current success, and future' (Croser 1979).

I have reread the paper I presented in 1979 in preparation for this event. Thank goodness wisdom accrues with experience.

The paper examined the economic drivers of the Australian table-wine boom from the 1960s, led by red wine until 1970 when two bottles of red were consumed for each bottle of white. This ratio was spectacularly reversed to four bottles of white to one of red by 1979.

The year 1979 was the apotheosis of Riesling as a variety in Australia before the onslaught of Chardonnay and, with the help of 'bag in box' white wine—also called Riesling—the real (Rhine) Riesling was a significant driver of the 18 per cent growth of domestic white wine sales in 1978–79. This dramatic wine colour preference reversal had a major detrimental economic effect on the red wine planted and stocked industry, prescient to the effects of the collapse of the international premium Australian red wine market after the 1996–2004 red grape planting boom.

The 1979 paper did predict the move to Chardonnay: 'In the quality area a movement away from the simplicity of perfectly made alcoholic fruit juice [Riesling and Traminer,] to more complex styles is becoming evident with Chardonnay leading the way.'

In these very early days of Chardonnay in Australia nobody could have predicted that Chardonnay would become the globe's dominant branded commodity wine variety as well as being an important fine wine variety.

Since the end of the 1970s, Riesling has consistently lost market share, initially to the Chardonnay tsunami and afterwards to the lemonade of Sauvignon Blanc and latterly to inoffensive Pinot Gris.

Ironically at the 1979 Symposium, Helmut Becker, the great Professor of Viticulture from the Geisenheim Institute, gave a paper called 'Anatomy of a good German white wine from grape to glass' (Becker 1979).

Professor Becker focused on the increased productivity of German vineyards from 20 to 100 hectolitres per hectare (15 tonnes/ha) due to clonal selection, and on the burgeoning success of German white wine in export markets to the detriment of the domestic market.

This was just before the collapse of the German export market for white wine in the 1980s—largely attributed to the dilution of quality and the predominant use of high-yielding Muller Thurgau rather than Riesling.

Despite its market share demise, Riesling has always retained the admiration of the finer wine influencers and attracts a disproportionate amount of fine wine press, which just doesn't convert to mass market sales.

That is in its way understandable and I hope to make the case that Riesling can only be produced in restricted quantities from specially suited areas and that it doesn't make mass market appealing wine outside of those areas. Riesling doesn't have the ubiquitous geographic range of Chardonnay for the production of branded commodity wine. That's to Riesling's long-term advantage.

My views on Canberra as a Riesling district are well known from my chairmanship of the Regional Wine Show. Everything you want to know about 'Riesling in Australia' is contained in the book called just that, edited by Ken Helm and Trish Burgess (2010). Ken has taken deliberate delight in quoting my response to the best Rieslings of the 2009 Canberra Regional Wine Show as being 'world class'. In the biologically complex and variable world of fine wine, Riesling and Canberra are a compass point.

That's to the Canberra wine region's long-term advantage.

Riesling is widely described as a 'noble grape' and, in the words of passionate Riesling advocate Jancis Robinson MW, 'Riesling is so clearly one of the world's great vines, arguably that which produces the finest white wines of all' (Robinson 1986).

For humans, the word noble connotes certain attributes, which are defined by genetics, a superiority of bearing and gallantry of action, which relate to the highest class of society, the so-called aristocrats. Let's hope Riesling lives up to its noble reputation better than that privileged group.

Getting away from the anthropomorphic approach to grape nobility, attributes of nobility for grape varieties could be

- consistent production of high-quality wine of unique varietal character
- in response to defined terroirs
- recorded over multiple centuries
- consistently attracting premium prices
- for wines that age for a long time
- creating high capital value for those vineyards that are especially suited to growing the variety.

Riesling ticks most of these boxes.

It enhances the noble image if the origins of the variety are shrouded in legend and the mystery and intrigue of a journey to Europe from somewhere in the Levant in a Crusader's swag.

Riesling's origins are much more prosaic.

Modern genetic analysis has established Riesling and Chardonnay are half-siblings with a common mother, the Hunnic variety Gouais Blanc. Whereas Chardonnay's father has been established as Pinot Noir, Riesling's father has evaded certain identification but could have been a wild form of Traminer (Jancis Robinson, Personal communication, 2011).

The French medieval ampelographers divided their grape varieties into the common, called 'Hunnic', and the noble, called 'Frankish'. The Franks' view of themselves and the Huns across the Rhine prevailed then as now and was anthropomorphised to grape varieties. Riesling, Pinot Noir, Pinot Gris and Traminer were *Frankish* (Chardonnay didn't exist until the seventeenth century), but the mother of the two contenders for the most noble white variety, Guoias Blanc, was a well-travelled, promiscuous *Hunnic* commoner identified as the parent of at least 80 other existing varieties.

Riesling was first identified in German documentation in the fifteenth century and was well established as the noble variety of the Rhine by the early eighteenth century.

In Australia Riesling was certainly among the importation of cuttings directly from Europe in 1832 by James Busby (1833) and the Macarthurs at Camden Park (1838) and was probably included in importations before 1832.

Whenever and however it arrived in all viticultural corners of Australia, Riesling was identified consistently and very early in Australian viticulture as the superior-performing white grape variety among the hundreds imported.

The best documentation of Riesling's early viticultural performance are the collections of articles written for the SA *Advertiser* and the Melbourne *Age* by Ebenezer Ward, under the titles of the *Vineyards and Orchards of South Australia, 1862* (1862) and the *Vineyards of Victoria as Visited by Ebenezer Ward in 1864* (1864).

Eleven of the 42 vineyards Ward visited in South Australia had Riesling and of these all but one were in the Adelaide/Barossa hills. It was already apparent to South Australia's early viticulturists that Riesling excelled in cool climates more similar to its native Rhineland.

In Victoria Ward visited only the cool regions around Geelong, Bendigo and Ballarat and there 21 of the 71 vineyards had Riesling.

Ward's comments about an 1852 Riesling from Pewsey Vale and an 1857 Riesling from Evandale—both vineyards in the high country adjacent to Angaston—are prescient about the future of Australian Riesling in that and similar cool areas: 'Here [at Pewsey Vale], as at Evandale, we consider the choicest wine to be the Riesling, thoroughly matured, fragrant, delicate and pure.'

The Pewsey Vale wine was 10 years old when tasted.

It is easy in hindsight to see why Riesling excelled amongst the early varietal imports into Australia.

Viticulturally it is of moderate vigour, hardy and is reliably fruitful. Oenologically it produces grapes of moderate sugar, high acid and low pH. In these early days of primitive winemaking, these were essential compositional characteristics to ensure complete and clean fermentations and the wine preservative qualities required for ageing.

Let's move from the past to the present and future of Riesling.

What do we know about Riesling now that will help us optimise this noble grape's future in Australia and Canberra in particular?

We know that Riesling character relies on the Muscat-related aromatic compounds, the mono and sesqui-terpenes, which are largely absent from Chardonnay and Sauvignon Blanc.

These are the floral (geraniums and roses) and citrus-smelling tertiary compounds, present at subtle levels and in synergistic combinations in Riesling, which give it such a delicate and fruity aroma.

Many of these compounds exist in an odourless state bound to glucose in juice and wine and this labile pool of flavours can be released by glycolisis.

We know these compounds are produced at different levels by different clones and we can select for the most expressive clones.

We know that the kerosene character (trimethyldihydronaphthalene, TDN) of ageing Riesling is formed from carotenes—the yellow pigment of white grapes—which are in turn formed in response to sunlight exposure of the berries and vine stress. Some like it; some don't.

This genetic and biochemical knowledge can help to refine the expression of Riesling quality wherever it is grown.

Much more importantly, we are now beginning to understand the terroir requirements for the best expressions of Riesling.

John Gladstones in his new masterly work, *Wine Terroir and Climate Change* (2011), places Riesling in both grape maturity group four, requiring 1200 degree-days to ripen for the low alcohol and sweeter 'classic styles', and in group five, requiring 1260 degree-days or more for the traditional Australian fuller-bodied dry styles.

His ambivalence about the suitable climate for Riesling is fuelled by Riesling's ability to produce fine wine in Geisenheim at 1045 degree-days and at Clare at 1777 degree-days. Nobody disputes the qualities of these very different Riesling styles.

Elsewhere it has been noted that Riesling best expresses its qualities in a climate with a high daily range (day/night) of temperature.

That is partially true but Geisenheim has a daily range of only 9.8°C and Clare 15°C.

It seems more likely that Riesling responds well in warmer climates only if the diurnal range is high and the cooling effect of night is strong enough to trap acid and retain the delicacy of fruit quality.

A graph of well-respected Riesling terroirs around the world demonstrates that cool terroirs do have low to moderate daily ranges and that the only successful warm-to-hot Riesling terroirs have high daily ranges. The correlation is strong and Canberra fits in the upper end of the ideal curve at 1441 degree-days and 14.2°C daily range (Gladstones 1992).

Climate might be the primary determinant of a successful Riesling terroir but geology and soil are also very important.

The great Riesling terroirs are largely on the older hard rocks—Cambrian and pre-Cambrian gneisses, schists, slates and granites—on the Rhine and Mosel in

Germany, on the Danube in Austria and in most Australian successful Riesling terroirs. There are exceptions of Riesling on Jurassic and post–limestone-based soils in Germany, Alsace, the Clare Valley and in Waipara, New Zealand.

In the words of Helmut Becker (1979): 'In stony acid soils we get more elegant wines, whereas in heavy soils [limestone marls] we get wines with full body.'

The limestone-based Rieslings are lower in acid, softer and less delicate in character than those from the slates and granites. This is particularly true of the wines from the dolomitic limestone of the lower Clare Valley versus the wines from the slate of the upper Clare Valley. Some of this is physiologically driven because of the exchange of different cations across the roots of the vine, some is due to the different light and heat-reflective, absorptive and re-radiation properties of the two rock types.

Riesling is genetically a low to moderate vigour vine and the vigour limiting nature of limestone soils tends to tip Riesling vines into the imbalance of higher crops and lower leaf photosynthetic capacity detracting from quality.

Happily, the Canberra region seems to provide the slightly acidic soils from shales to allow Riesling to best express its varietal excellence.

Riesling is the most versatile of white varieties within its suited terroir range. In addition to the traditional moderate alcohol (12–13 per cent), dry (<7.5 gpl sugar), moderate acid (7 gpl), fresh and flavoursome Rieslings from Mount Barker/Frankland, WA, Clare Valley, Eden Valley, Great Western, Heywood/Drumborg and Canberra, there is a new generation of Rieslings from cooler climates in the Adelaide Hills, Tasmania and New Zealand. These are harvested fully ripe at lower sugar, higher acid and lower pH than their traditional Australian counterparts. They are more likely to reflect the fruit-enhancing effect of *Botrytis* and are being made to lower alcohol and higher residual sugar levels. These wines and those of Oregon, the Mosel/Saar/Ruwer and Rhine are delicious and they serve a purpose in modern life as lower-alcohol, refreshing aperitifs or just to drink with an apple under a tree on Sunday afternoon.

I think it is a mistake to try to make this style from early harvested grapes from the warmer traditional dry Riesling wine regions of Australia such as Clare, Eden Valley and Canberra.

Finally, as an optimistic aside, Riesling consumption is growing strongly in the United States, led by the wines of the cool/warm desert climate of the Yakima Valley to the east of the Cascades in Washington State. A very high daily range of 17.2°C and a moderate heat summation of 1379 degree-days allow the production of 'off-dry' wines with full, fresh flavours—sort of a hybrid of traditional Australian and Alsatian.

Down the coast to the west of the Cascades in a much wetter and cooler climate (1191 degree-days) and lower daily range (10.4°C) in the Willamette Valley, Oregon, Riesling has the lower alcohol, higher acid and sweeter profile of the German, Tasmanian and New Zealand wines.

I have not addressed the many winemaking variations visited on Riesling in the cause of in-market differentiation.

The real source of Riesling quality and style is the terroir in which it is grown and the quality of the viticultural management; however, it is common oenological knowledge that Riesling requires delicate handling, low phenol extraction, cool anaerobic fermentation and storage and that it doesn't respond well to oak treatment. Australian winemakers have led the world in defining the way to get the best out of their Riesling fruit.

When Dr A. C. Kelly wrote his marvellous treatise on winemaking called *Wine-Growing in Australia* (1867), Riesling was definitely one of the noble varieties on his mind when he wrote: 'In the great diversity of soil and climate to be found in Australia, there is little doubt that every variety cultivated in Europe would somewhere find a suitable location in which to develop its most valued qualities.'

I am sure he would not have been thinking of Canberra as a suitable location for Riesling at the time but if he were alive today I am equally sure he would not be surprised by the evident synergy between Canberra and the noble Riesling variety.

References

Australian Wine and Brandy Producers, 1980, *The Australian Wine and Brandy Producing Industry—Quantity of grapes crushed: By variety: 1979 vintage.*

Becker, Helmut, 1979, Anatomy of a good German white wine from grape to glass, Third Wine Symposium, University House, The Australian National University, Canberra.

Busby, James, 1833, *Journal of a Tour through Some of the Vineyards of Spain and France*, [1979 facsimile reprint], The David Ell Press.

Croser, Brian, 1979, Australian white wines—their history, current success, and future, Third Wine Symposium, University House, The Australian National University, Canberra.

Gladstones, John, 1992, *Viticulture and Environment*, Winetitles, Adelaide.

Gladstones, John, 2011, *Wine Terroir and Climate Change*, Wakefield Press, Adelaide.

Helm, Ken and Burgess, Trish, 2010, *Riesling in Australia*, Winetitles, Adelaide.

Kelly, A. C., 1867 [1980], *Winegrowing in Australia*, [Facsimile reprint], The David Ell Press.

Robinson, Jancis, 1986, *Vines, Grapes and Wine*, Mitchell Beazley.

Ward, Ebenezer, 1862, *Vineyards and Orchards of South Australia 1862*, [1979 facsimile reprint], Sullivans Cove.

Ward, Ebenezer, 1864, *The Vineyards of Victoria as Visited by Ebenezer Ward in 1864*, [1980 facsimile reprint], Sullivans Cove.

12. Shiraz: Past, present and future

Dan Buckle
Mount Langi Ghiran Winery

Tim Kirk from Clonakilla and his brother Kiaran asked me to come here today to talk about Shiraz. This was for two reasons: first, because as winemaker at Mount Langi Ghiran I am producing about 700 tonnes of Shiraz each vintage—and this is our specialisation.

Second, because I recently wrote a blog piece where I criticised some Australian Shiraz producers for using the synonym Syrah on their labels. Wonderful thing about blogs is that anyone can post them. Frightening thing about blogs is that apparently some people actually read them.

So I'm interested in etymology and words from my past life as an arts student, and so a little more on that later.

But first I want to give you a snapshot of where Shiraz is currently sitting in the Australian wine landscape. The title suggests 'past, present and future', but chronological order seems a bit simplistic so we'll start with the present.

Shiraz is Australia's most planted grape, in terms of hectares and production in tonnes. With more than 44 000 ha of Shiraz planted in Australia in 2009, this single variety represents more than 28 per cent of Australia's vineyard area and nearly 44 per cent of Australia's red wine crush.

Nearly half the red wine made in Australia in 2009 was Shiraz. Plantings of this variety in this country are nearly 15 000 ha greater than the next two varieties, Chardonnay and Cabernet Sauvignon.

In this country, Shiraz is king, at least so far.

The reason for this dominance is less than exciting, however, and a little more pragmatic, since for the most part Shiraz is grown for its reliability, yield, moderate ripening period and tolerance to heat more than for its more romantic strengths. Unfettered by the appellative regulations they have in Europe, here market forces have been responsible for the rise of Shiraz to this position.

The result is that we now have Shiraz plantings all the way from east to west, and from north to south. There is Shiraz grown from the hills of southern Queensland to the Coal River Valley behind Hobart and all the way across all SA winegrowing areas.

In his book *The Botany of Desire*, Michael Pollan puts forward the case that certain plant species have domesticated humans for the propagation of their genomes. Pollan cites the examples of apples, potatoes, tulips and cannabis to support this idea that, by offering us certain highly desirable features, the plants are able to ensure that we humans keep their genes alive. In the case of wine grapes, the obvious attraction of readily fermentable fruits and microbially stable wines has led us humans to go to enormous lengths (not to mention financial ruin) to propagate this species. *Vinifera* is successful on this planet due to mankind. The same line of thinking works in particular to the specific set of genes we know as Shiraz.

We can look at Shiraz's dominance in Australian winegrowing in terms of viticulture and production. Shiraz is successful because it has a reasonable ripening period—not too late or too rapid—and yields well. And, above all else, with a little bit of winemaking skill, Shiraz can give us reliably what I call simply 'fruity red booze'.

Shiraz, in the form of fruity red booze, whether as a single variety or blended, forms the backbone of Australia's red commodity wine.

By commodity wine I mean the 95 per cent of Australian wine that is destined for retail shelves. Commodity wine is labelled usually by variety and brand. Commodity wine is sold largely on price not point of difference. And commodity wine can easily be swapped one for another; there is no unique selling proposition.

In restaurant terms, it's a little like comparing a trip to McDonald's with a trip to Tetsuya's. I know where I'd rather be.

But this is not the future, nor is it the point of excitement we find in this variety.

Instead, lovers of fine Shiraz know that Shiraz can be so much more than simply fruity. This is my big point and I don't need to emphasise this too much to Canberra winemakers.

Shiraz can be floral. Shiraz can be spicy. Shiraz can be peppery and/or savoury. In Shiraz, these nuances are what excite me.

Structurally, Shiraz can be massive or light bodied, monolithic and towering, or slippery and supple, or bold and brutish. Like Pinot Noir and Riesling, Shiraz responds brilliantly to its growing environment and maker. Shiraz fine wines—compared with their commodity namesakes—very often show true terroir.

But let's go back to the beginnings of Australia's great red grape.

Shiraz is a synonym widely accepted in Australia for the French word *Syrah*. Shiraz has a long history in Australia, dating back to the 1860s in my part of

Victoria, and earlier still with the Busby collection. James Busby's return to Europe from Australia in 1831 and subsequent importation into Australia of many, many *Vinifera* varieties brought the first Shiraz cuttings into New South Wales in 1832.

This was Busby's second trip to Europe, which brought Shiraz into Australia.

By 1839, Shiraz had found its way to South Australia. The oldest existing vineyards there go back to 1843. At the time, Busby was calling the variety 'Scyras' and 'Ciras', which were apparently misspellings of the French *Syrah*.

Through some linguistic morphing, and more than a little convincing (but entirely incorrect) folklore about the origins of Syrah in France, Australians long ago turned the word 'Scyras' into 'Shiraz'. Through this we have the current, dominant usage of this word.

Now Australia is a young country and we are sometimes a bit shy about our ability to generate vernacular. Indeed, typical Aussie words often carry baggage of being uncultured and uneducated. So perhaps it's not surprising that there is a growing trend in calling cool-climate Shiraz by the French name Syrah. Pretentious maybe, but *c'est la vie*. This is a cultural cringe thing that I would prefer to discourage.

In any case, the false histories of the word Shiraz are interesting and entertaining. Some suggest legends of Shiraz grapes finding their way to the Rhone from Iran's city of Shiraz. Others suggest the word Shiraz derives from Syracuse in Italy.

The links between the city of Shiraz in Iran, or Syracuse in Italy, and Syrah/Shiraz grapes are mythological only. These commonly accepted but incorrect faux etymologies of Shiraz/Syrah might indeed be simply a foolish acceptance of historical sophistry. Unfortunately, bullshit is extremely common in the world of wine, where people frequently posture as knowledgeable, and yet their poorly referenced and anecdotal evidence is frequently subjective and erroneous.

In the case of Shiraz/Syrah, the scientific truth is that these stories have been shown to be incorrect, both by classical ampelography and more recently by DNA.

DNA studies done on many *Vinifera* cultivars in 2000 indicate that Syrah is indeed the product of breeding Dureza and Mondeuse blanche.

Looking at the European history, there are classical references in the first century AD to wines made around the then city of Tegna—now Tain L'Hermitage—in the Rhone Valley. Pliny the Elder makes mention of a certain *Vinum picatum*, which translates to 'tarry wine', due to the wine's tarry flavours.

Syrah-growing in the Rhone was for the most part a local affair and managed by the local religious orders, until recent history.

Notably, in the nineteenth century, Hermitage became famous first as an addition to Bordelaise wines, where wines were often blended for volume or quality, and indeed occasionally labelled honestly as Hermitage. So whilst Australian winemakers have done wonderfully well from blending the Shiraz and Cabernet grapes, we cannot claim to have invented this idea. At least we have not sought to cover our tracks.

After the attacks of *Phylloxera* in the 1870s and the two world wars of the early twentieth century, the Syrah vineyards of the Northern Rhone were almost abandoned, with the exception of Hermitage. So the rise and rise of Northern Rhone wines is a recent business.

It's interesting to consider that Syrah in France has never had the noble, aristocratic status of Riesling, Chardonnay, Pinot Noir or Cabernet Sauvignon, and this indeed might be part of the reason this variety fits so well with Australia.

This low status might well appeal to our sense of humility and our down to earth identity.

Shiraz history in Australia, as I said before, goes back to the 1830s. Unlike the newcomer Chardonnay, Shiraz has been a part of the Australian viticultural landscape since the beginning. There are marvelous examples of Hunter Valley Shiraz from the 1930s and 1940s, which can still be found today, if you know where to look and if you like begging.

In the second half of the past century, the story of Australian fine wine is tightly linked to this variety, through Penfolds' Grange and Henschke's Hill of Grace, as well as through other great Shiraz wines, especially those from the Hunter Valley, central Victoria and South Australia. Australia boasts some of the oldest continual plantings of this variety anywhere in the world.

But the rise and rise of Shiraz in Australia has been for the most part due to the growth and international development of commodity wine. In the 1980s, the Australian wine industry grew rapidly from a relatively disjointed rural business to a leading producer, innovator and exporter playing in the global wine industry. Varietally labelled Shiraz and Shiraz blends have been integral to this success.

There were some tipping points along the way. The 1980s—the great decade of deregulation—saw the dollar float and the politics of Reagan and Thatcher come into play. British off-licence liquor laws were changed to permit sale of wine on supermarket shelves, opening up a new, mass channel. At the same time, the baby-boomer generation was making the move from beer and spirits to wine.

Clearly legible, English-language, honest varietal labels and strong branding enabled Australian Shiraz to gain very significant market share. This success was firmly based in the commodity wine sector and largely competed on price more than any specific point of difference.

But good things cannot last forever, and, as Michael Porter clearly points out, you cannot have a price-competitive strategy and a differentiation strategy at the same time.

Now, Australian wine is suffering the backlash of this, where we are seen by our overseas markets as industrial wine producers—cheap and cheerful, if not cheap and nasty.

Recent history in the past seven years has seen the increase in mergers and acquisitions across international boundaries, and the rise of the international conglomerates. Groups such as Pernod Ricard, Allied Domenq, Constellation, LVMH and Treasury Wine Estates have grown and grown, largely in response to this so-called 'commodification' of wine. Economies of scale and vertically integrated production and distribution systems have sought to overcome the agricultural challenges of season and supply, of rainfall and heatwave, through global capacity. Again, in Australia as in France, Shiraz has had a large role to play. But the long lead times and high capital inputs involved have meant that this style of industrialisation does not make for an easy fit.

The current situation for Australian Shiraz growers is tough. Pricing pressure and global competition are squeezing margins. The usual agricultural problems of weather, mildew, fire, drought and rain are compounded by global issues of financial crises, climate change and the potential demise of the American empire.

All this puts more pressure on the commodity market, where Shiraz has such a role to play. Not so bad for the fine wine market.

Now I know that you can say anything with statistics, and certainly the Wine Australia website has lots of them, but let me point to the example of Shiraz grape price in these different regions to give a snapshot of the trends. The problem with looking too closely at these data is you can easily get confused—for example, Canberra grape price is only for those grapes actually sold. I'm not sure if I could buy any grapes from Clonakilla (or Coldstream Hills, or Tapanappa), but if I even could the price would not be represented here. It would be much higher. We value Langi Shiraz grapes internally at $6000 per tonne.

Table 1 Shiraz Crush

Year	1999	2004	2009
Tonnes ('000)	197	438	394
Price	$1338	$892	$750 (est.)

Source: Halliday (2010), 2011 Wine Companion, <http://www.wineaustralia.com>

Table 2 Shiraz Price (per Tonne) by Region

Year	1999	2002	2005	2008
Inland I.A.	$1056	$727	$497	$609
Barossa	$1919	$1959	$1304	$1736
Yarra Valley	$2136	$1761	$1644	$1989
Canberra	N/A	$1685	$1795	$1817

Source: <http://www.wineaustralia.com>

Tonnes produced grew between 1999 and 2004, and since then has been relatively stable, given the variability of agriculture. But this static situation of tonnage and hectares is misleading, and does not reflect market demand.

Price per tonne gives us a better indication, and it does point to a trend. This shows the average grape price for Shiraz has been steadily falling. But this is not the whole story.

Commodity Shiraz grape prices have fallen, in the inland areas of Riverland, Riverina and Murray–Darling, by just more than $1050 per tonne in 1999 to below $600 over the years 2001 to 2008. Since vintage 2008, global financial crises only make the situation worse. And in some cases these prices are skewed unrealistically high due to frost and drought.

I'm painting an ugly picture but it's a state of affairs that the Australian wine industry needs to acknowledge. It's also a situation that people like Brian Croser and James Halliday have been warning the Australian Shiraz growers about for almost a decade.

But it gets even worse for commodity Shiraz growers when we consider the problems associated with climate change, increasing temperatures, increasing heatwave events and changes in rainfall patterns.

Unfortunately, the rain and mildew events of the past six months will prolong this circumstance by artificially inflating the price and market because of demand. For growers who have survived the past season, this puts off the inevitable point that commodity grape-growing in Australia has a limit that is much, much smaller than it has been in the past.

I recently met a Shiraz grower in Swan Hill who was talking about replacing his grapevines—with pumpkins. Seriously. Probably a good idea.

The more positive and exciting trends are the stability and growth in value of cool-climate Shiraz grapes.

If the value of grapes per tonne is indicative of future trends then cool-climate Shiraz growers, and high-quality Shiraz growers from all parts, still have good cause for optimism.

Some other good news is that for this financial year, for Mount Langi Ghiran, for the first time our export sales in Asia will overtake our export sales in all other markets. This is by volume, by revenue and by margin. I suspect we are not alone.

Our current success in Asia is largely because we took the decision four years ago to stop punching it out on the retail shelves in the United Kingdom and Scandinavia, and to invest time and effort in China and South-East Asia instead.

So I want to finish talking about what I love in Shiraz, and why the future is not too cloudy.

The future is not too cloudy because we have an economic powerhouse on our doorstep and solid domestic demand.

But most importantly for wine lovers, we have the rise and rise of fine-wine Shiraz. And fine-wine Shiraz has nuance, subtlety, variety, diversity…it can smell of violets and ginger, pepper and exotic spices, dense fruits. Its diversity in flavours and structures can match any number of meals. So for drinking pleasure, I think the future of Australian Shiraz might not be cheap, but certainly won't be nasty.

13. Emerging and Alternative Varieties: Considerations, challenges and choices

Libby Tassie
Tassie Viticultural Consulting

The area of alternative and emerging varieties is an optimistic and exciting part of the industry. This paper will look at the reasons for consideration of alternative varieties and at the challenges and choices involved in the decision making. Some of the material comes from the *Alternative Varieties Research to Practice* workshop book that I co-authored with Dr Peter Dry and Marcel Essling from the Australian Wine Research Institute.

Introduction

The definition of an alternative variety given by the Australian Alternative Varieties Wine Show (AAVWS) is any variety other than Cabernet Sauvignon, Chardonnay, Chenin Blanc, Colombard, Grenache, Merlot, Pinot Noir, Sauvignon Blanc, Semillon, Shiraz, Riesling and Verdelho…and Pinot Grigio as of 2010. This definition is a changing one—for example, in the 1970s Chardonnay was considered to be an alternative or unusual variety; in the 1990s it was Pinot Gris; and now Vermentino and Fiano, among others, are the new alternatives.

Over this time there have been a number of steadfast champions of alternative varieties, such as Brown Brothers, Yalumba, Mark Lloyd (Coriole) and Gary Crittenden, who have trialled and promoted new varieties to the industry. In the past decade in particular, there has been a significant increase in the production of alternative varieties. An important impetus was the importation of 70 clones and varieties in the late 1990s by Bruce Chalmers (Chalmers Nursery) with Rod Bonfiglioli.

There are a huge number of varieties around the world: more than 10 000 named varieties in international germplasm collections, with this number estimated to be reduced to about 5000 following DNA fingerprinting identification in the process of sorting out varieties known under different names. Recent studies have also shown large numbers of unique or autochthonous varieties in regions of Europe—for example, 28 just in the southern Italian region of Calabria (Schneider et al. 2009).

There is increasing interest in alternative varieties due to globalisation, with greater travel and awareness by winemakers and viticulturists, as well as by consumers. In addition, improved winemaking and viticulture techniques have shown the true potential of some varieties over the past 20–30 years. Some varieties were also poorly acknowledged historically, as traditionally many European wines were identified by region rather than varietal make-up.

Considerations

Some considerations for a producer when looking at adopting alternative varieties include the changing market, changing climate, climate suitability, viticultural and winemaking characteristics and the practicalities of the time required to put the wine on the shelf; marketing is a significant topic that will not be covered here.

Changing Markets

As Phil Ruthven outlined in the Fourteenth Australian Wine Industry Technical Conference (Adelaide, 2010), the traditional markets of the United States and the United Kingdom are changing, with Asia becoming more prominent. There is also a general increasing interest in different flavours and lower-alcohol wines in the marketplace.

Climate Change and Implications

Implications of climate change include increasing temperatures and thus changing environments for grape-growing. In Canberra, for example, the current mean January temperature (MJT) of 20.4°C is predicted to increase by 0.3 to 1.2°C by 2030 and 0.6 to 2.9°C by 2050 (Leanne Webb, Personal communication).

There are also implications for phenology, with earlier budburst and earlier and warmer harvest and a subsequent compression of harvest, as well as more extreme weather events and higher carbon dioxide concentrations. These will have impacts on vine growth and quality and also on management logistics. One of the adaptation options to climate change is to use new varieties, either to cope with greater heat in warmer regions or as an addition to the varietal portfolio in cooler climates where they previously were not able to ripen. Some varieties that might show more heat and drought tolerance are the two southern Italian red varieties Nero d'Avola and Negro Amaro. Adequate ripening of some of the later-maturing varieties such as Aglianico, Nero d'Avola and Montepulciano might need to be trialled in cooler regions such as Canberra. Use of early ripeners such as Savagnin, Albarino and Gruner Veltliner also has the advantage of reduced water use.

Climate Suitability

Consideration needs to be given to the climate of origin and the suitability of the variety in the new climate—that is, homoclime assessment, which can be quite a complex area. Typical temperature indices used are MJT (or mean July temperature in the northern hemisphere) and heat degree-days (HDD) or growing degree-days (GDD)—that is, the effective heat days per month in the growing season. However, these do not distinguish regions by continentality—that is, the difference between the warmest and coolest months of the year. Further consideration is given to this topic by McKay et al. (1999) and Gladstones (1992, 2011).

The challenges of equating regions with just MJT data, for example, are illustrated in Table 1, which looks at regional climatic comparisons. This illustrates the differences in regions that might have equal MJT—for example, Turin and Mildura—but significantly different ripening season temperatures and GDD. Canberra and Turin, with close GDD, have very different MJT and continentalities, thus different temperature regimes during berry ripening stages.

Table 1 Regional Climatic Comparisons, Looking at MJT in Degrees Celsius, Temperature Two and Three Months after the MJT, GDD in Degrees Celsius and continentality.

Region	MJT	2 months + (3 months)	GDD	Conti[1]
Rioja, Spain	21.3	18.7 (13.7)	1386	
Sienna, Chianti	23.6	19.9 (14.3)	1477	18.3
Turin, Piedmont	23.7	19.4 (12.8)	1429	23.3
Ararat	20.5	17.3 (13.5)	1335	11.7
Clare	21.3	19.2 (14.8)	1594	13.3
Mildura	23.3	20.9 (16.2)	2244	13.7 (Mer)[2]
Canberra	20.4	17.6 (13.0)	1424	14.7
Coonawarra	19.3	17.4 (14.5)	1337	10.1 (Kyb)[3]

1 Conti refers to continentality.
2 (Mer) refers to data from Merbein.
3 (Kyb) refers to data from Kybybolite.
Source: Dry and Coombe (2004); Gladstones (1992).

When looking at overseas climatic data, location of the climate station and the elevation of the vineyards need to be taken into account, as there is a decrease of 0.6° per 100 m of altitude that might not be reflected in available weather station data, as they are often located at sea level. For example, the white variety Fiano is grown between 300 and 400 m at Avellino outside Naples in southern Italy and Agiorgitiko, a red Greek variety, is grown in the Nemea region at 450–650 m.

Another consideration is whether the region of origin is the optimal location for the variety—that is, is the variety versatile? Chardonnay was originally grown in a very narrow climatic range in Europe, but has proven to be very versatile, performing well in a range of regions. Aglianico is grown in one region in Italy but initial wine from Langhorne Creek and the Riverina in Australia indicates it might be more versatile. Regional trials are really required to answer this question.

Viticultural Characteristics

Viticultural characteristics to consider are phenology (budburst and harvest timing), susceptibility to pests and diseases, growth characteristics (vigour, growth habit and bunch structure), adaptability (to climate, soils and rootstocks), suitability to mechanisation and fruit composition (acid, pH and potential quality). The main limiting factor for regions such as Canberra is a relatively short growing season and spring frosts, so late budburst and early to midseason ripening varieties would be most likely to succeed.

Winemaking Characteristics

Overseas, many varieties are typically blended. Sangiovese in Chianti Classico is blended with a maximum of 20 per cent other varieties, Tempranillo in Rioja is generally blended with Grenache, Mazuela, Graciano and Viura, and, in Sicily, the DOC wine Cerasuolo de Vittoria is made from Nero d'Avola and at least 40 per cent Frappato. In Australia, winemaking trials and varietal assessment are generally only on the single variety, which might be limiting the true potential of a variety. Tempranillo is one example of a variety that people are now trialling in blends. Winemaking characteristics to consider include susceptibility to oxidation and wine composition—that is, tannins, phenolics and colour—that might differ from varieties with which we are familiar. The white varieties of Verdejo from Spain and Assyrtiko from Greece typically have problems of oxidation and require non-oxidative handling. Some reds—for example, Aglianico—have good tannin and aroma but low colour in comparison with Shiraz or Cabernet; this is a phenomena with which producers of Nebbiolo will be familiar.

Challenges

Information

There are more sources of information from both overseas and Australia emerging as interest in varietals increases. Peter Dry has compiled a list of monographs, websites and periodicals available on the GWRDC website. More comparative data on varietal performance would be useful, as it is sometimes difficult to equate interpretation of disease susceptibility, for example. For comparative Australian information there is only one varietal trial, at Manjumup in Western Australia, with another trial being planted in a second climatic region of that State. Some regional groups are collating and providing information on the performance of alternative varieties in their regions—for example, Riverland Alternative Variety Group with a particular focus on Vermentino and Adelaide Hills Vine Improvement with a focus on Gruner Veltliner.

Ensuring Varietal Trueness to Type and Correct Naming

It is critical to ensure that the alternative variety is true to type and to avoid costly mistakes such as the recent Albarino/Savagnin Blanc debacle. This mistake affected nurseries, growers and producers, with up to 50 producers affected, some contracts cancelled or the price per tonne significantly reduced, and marketing strategies had to be adjusted. This experience has dramatically highlighted the importance of ensuring varietal identity is verified by DNA fingerprinting and/or ampelographic inspection.

Recent interest in Grenache Blanc has revealed via DNA testing that some vines assumed to be Grenache Blanc in South Australia were in fact Biancone—a mistake first flagged by Truel in 1976 (Antcliff 1976).

There are now commercial DNA testing facilities in France, the United States and Australia. In the development of the DNA database, it is important to use ampelographically verified reference vines, which still needs to be done with the Australian collections. There is currently a small-scale coordinated Variety Verification Project partly funded by GWRDC, Wine Australia, some vine-improvement bodies, nurseries and VINA, which aims to ensure via DNA testing that some of the alternative varieties currently being planted are indeed true to type.

The use of synonyms in Europe can be confusing; the variety of Vermentino, for example, is known as Rolle in Provence, Pigato in some parts of Liguria, Favorita in Piedmont and Malvoisie in Corsica. Nero d'Avola of Sicily is also known as Calabrese in Calabria.

When exporting wines, the varietal name on the Australian section of the OIV list of wine varieties and synonyms must be used. Some names, however, are not permitted in Europe due to the protection of geographical indications, such as Prosecco and Montepulciano.

Time Required to Develop a New Variety

Development of a new variety takes time. The planting material might be in the country or might need to be imported, with quarantine processing taking about two years. Getting the vineyard into production and to second crop has been estimated by Brown Brothers to take nine years, if importation is required, and more than five years if the material is already in the country (Walpole 2008). With wine production and trials, the time to get a new variety on the shelf could be at least seven to 10 years.

The development of a new variety, however, is no guarantee of success. After trying to ensure the correct site, appropriate vineyard management practices to optimise production and winemaking to produce the required wine style, the wine still has to sell!

Choices

To determine the options available after some research the ultimate answer lies in onsite trials. The good news for cool climates under predicted climate change scenarios is that they expand the varietal possibilities. For the Canberra region the viticultural requirements are for the varieties to ripen adequately and avoid spring frosts—that is, to use late budburst, early to midseason ripening varieties.

In his recent book, Gladstones (2011) has compiled a list of grape maturity groups and estimated maturity dates for Canberra (Table 2). It is assumed anything in the later maturity groups of eight and nine would not currently ripen. The ability of the varieties to ripen depends also on aspect, altitude, soil type, and so on, and can vary somewhat from this table—for example, Sangiovese ripens before Cabernet Sauvignon in parts of the Barossa Valley.

Table 2 Grape Maturity Groups and Estimated Maturity Dates for Canberra.

Maturity group	Effec °C days	Varieties	Est. date reached
1	1020		27 Feb
2	1080		6 Mar
3	1140	Chard, Gewürztraminer	13 Mar
4	1200	G. Veltliner, Riesling	21 Mar
5	1260	Arneis, Shiraz	20 Mar
6	1320	Cab Sauv, Sangiovese	10 Apr
7	1380	Garganega, Carmenere, Graciano Nebbiolo	30 Apr
8	1440	Montepulciano, Aglianico	-
9	1500	Negro Amaro	-

Source: Gladstones (2011).

White Varieties

There are obviously more options for early ripening with white varieties. Some alternative whites that are currently being planted in Australia are Gruner Veltliner, Fiano, Arneis, Vermentino, Prosecco, Savagnin and Gargenega. This paper will look at just a few of these.

Gruner Veltliner

Gruner Veltliner is the most widely planted variety in Austria. The wines can be full bodied with complex aromas and characteristics of spice, pepper, apple, pear, pineapple and quince, fruit and savoury. Styles vary with region, climate and winemaking in Austria. In Australia there are six producers including Lark Hill in Canberra and Hahndorf Hill Winery in the Adelaide Hills, according to the *Australian and New Zealand Wine Industry Directory, 2011*.

It has early budburst and ripening, tends to be vigorous, has a good tolerance of *Botrytis* and is not particularly susceptible to downy or powdery mildews. Table 3 shows relative ripening dates and fruit composition at harvest from two wineries in different regions.

Table 3 Budburst and Harvest Data for Gruner Veltliner and Chardonnay in Canberra and the Adelaide Hills.

Variety	Budburst	Har	Be	pH	TA	t/ha
Chardonnay: Canberra Lark Hill	5 Oct	5 Apr	12.2	3.2	8.7	5.0
Gruner Veltliner: Canberra Lark Hill	12 Oct	15 Apr	12.5	3.3	8.2	3
Gruner Veltliner: Adelaide Hills; Hahndorf Hill	As Chard	Mid Mar	11.5	3.3	6.9	3.5

Source: Sue Carpenter, Lark Hill, and Larry Jacobs, Hahndorf Hill, Personal communications.

Fiano

Fiano is a very old white variety from the southern region of Campania, Italy, grown at altitudes of between 300 and 500 m. The Fiano d'Avellino has been shown to be different from the Fiano and Minutolo from Bari. The wine has appealing texture and great freshness—like fresh viognier, pomme fruits, florals and honey (Mark Lloyd; Anon. 2010). Fiano has midseason budburst and early to mid ripening—late for a white variety—and retains high acidity. In Australia there are 26 producers—up 63 per cent from 2010—for example, Ducks in a Row, Coriole and Chalmers.

Arneis

Arneis is one of Italy's distinctive white wines from Piedmont in the north of the country. The wine can be made into a range of styles with a variety of aromas and fruit—for example, peach, almonds and pears. It has early budburst and early to midseason ripening. The vine tends to be quite fruitful and vigorous with thick-skinned berries.

Vermentino

Vermentino is a white variety found in Liguria, Sardinia, Piedmont, Italy, and Corsica and Provence in France under various synonyms. The wine is aromatic, with crisp, dry, lemony acidity and minerality. It has early to midseason budburst with midseason ripening and is high yielding. There are 41 producers in Australia—an increase of 58 per cent from 2010.

Savagnin

Savagnin is grown in France, northern Italy and Austria. The wine has Riesling-like acidity and citrus, a Pinot Gris-like palate with a crisp, spicy finish (Darren Golding, Personal communication) and was favourably equated to Albarino when it was known under that name. It has early season budburst with early to midseason ripening and is generally a robust variety to grow. In Australia there are 35-plus producers—for example, Tscharke, Crittenden and Golding Wines.

Red Varieties

Tempranillo

Tempranillo is possibly about to emerge out of the alternative variety category in Australia. It is widely grown in Spain and Portugal, and makes great young wines, aged wines and fortified wines. The flavour of the wine has been described as a cross between Cabernet Sauvignon and Pinot Noir with wonderful fruit.

It has early season budburst, early to mid-season ripening and tends to have low acidity. There have been reports of sensitivity to drought. In Australia there are currently 286 producers—up 45 per cent from 2010—for example, Mt Majura, Yalumba and Crabtree Watervale.

Dolcetto

Dolcetto is from Piedmont, northern Italy. The wine is medium bodied, fresh, deep-crimson red, with typical cherry flavours, and often prunes and liquorice. It has early season budburst and early to midseason ripening. It might need careful management with crop and shoot thinning and possibly early harvest to avoid bunch split. Australia has 38 producers, including Bests (where it was known as Malbec) and Crittenden.

Sagrantino

Sagrantino is from Umbria, central Italy. The wine has great structure, high colour, phenols and tannins, with forest fruits, violets and vanilla (Walpole 2008). It has mid to late-season budburst and mid to late-season ripening. In Australia there are 12 producers including Coriole, Olivers and Chalmers.

What Will the Canberra Region Produce in 2050?

With current predictions of climate change, does one's planning include a gradual changing of the varietal mix, as ability to ripen expands the possibilities? This could include planting Tempranillo and Dolcetto now, Sagrantino in 10 years, and later-maturing varieties such as Nero d'Avola and Aglianico in 30 years.

Conclusion

Interest in alternative varieties is increasing in Australia, and it appears that there is great potential in the current economic and climatic environment—a changing scenario. We have some information about the varieties, but to assist good, informed decision making by growers, Australia needs more comparative information and trials in regions established to determine the best fit for these new varieties. There is no guarantee of success in the development of a new variety, and careful consideration and research as to the appropriate variety for a specific area still need to be undertaken.

References

Anonymous, 2010, 'Fiano', *Australia New Zealand Wine Industry Journal*, vol. 14, no. 4, pp. 69–73.

Antcliff, A. J., 1976, 'Variety identification in Australia. A French expert looks at our vines', *The Australian Grapegrower & Winemaker*.

Dry, P. R. and Dry, N. S., 2010, Emerging varieties from the Mediterranean workshop, Fourteenth AWITC, Adelaide.

Dry, P. R. and Coombe, B. G., 2004, *Viticulture. Volume 1: Resources*, [Second edition], Winetitles, Adelaide.

Gladstones, J., 1992, *Viticulture and Environment*, Winetitles, Adelaide.

Gladstones, J., 2011, *Wine, Terroir and Climate Change*, Wakefield Press, Adelaide.

McKay, A. D., Crittenden, G. J., Dry, P. R. and Hardie, W. J., 1999, *Italian Winegrape Varieties in Australia: Exploring the potential of Barbera, Nebbiolo, Sangiovese, Vernaccia di San Gimignano, Dolcetto and Arneis*, Winetitles, Adelaide.

Schneider, A. et al., 2009, 'Contributo all'identificazione dei principali vitigni', *Calabrese Frutticoltura*, nos 1–2, pp. 46–55.

Tassie, L., Dry, P. R. and Essling, M., 2010, *Alternative Varieties: Emerging options for a changing environment. Research to practice*, AWRI, Australia.

Walpole, M., 2008, The viticultural challenges of alternative varieties, Presentation to Queensland College of Wine and Tourism, <http://www.dpi.qld.gov.au/cps/>

14. Great Australian Wine: Are there any alternatives?

Nick Stock

My umbrella point hovers over the issue of alternative varieties and that the Canberra District wine region has such a lucky opportunity it cannot afford to squander. It has some important choices to make. Success is at stake.

Canberra has established Riesling and Shiraz with impressive speed and conviction; it's almost a dream come true and not just for the region's stakeholders. It's something to be celebrated. It has the attention of all enthusiasts, amateurs, dabblers, dilettantes, practitioners, experts and observers (and anyone else who happens to be in earshot) and now it must act to galvanise this attention.

My message for Canberra producers is to focus on their core mission first and foremost because timing is imperative to success and the moment is *now*. If they don't focus enough or well enough, the moment will pass. It will be harder to recreate the opportunity down the track.

Many (probably most) wine regions in Australia are struggling to identify, agree and focus collectively on their signature wines, as well as make them in sufficient enough numbers to be utterly convincing to the rest of the world.

Canberra has, through the work of the Edgar Rieke/John Kirk generation and subsequently the Tim Kirk/Ken Helm/Alex McKay/Nick O'Leary/Brian Martin and son generation, elaborated a compelling terroir. They've identified a clear opportunity to realise signature styles that are undoubtedly great wines in a world sense. They're interesting, distinctive and can be made consistently.

This presents a significant opportunity. Throwing the seemingly boundless 'excitement' of alternative varieties into the mix could be a liability for the region at this moment in their brief and to-date successful history, and so mine is a cautionary tale.

More than that though, I also make the point that the act of sourcing, growing, making and bottling a wine is something anyone can do; but success dictates that the mission for Canberra's winemakers is to make great and distinctive wine. We actually don't have any need for anything else. We have enough wine in the world already—in fact, we have way too much.

We have too much bulk wine in tanks, we have too much average wine, we have too much of the wrong type of wine, the wrong style, labelled, in cleanskin, we have too much okay wine, we even have too much pretty darn decent wine. But we have a shortage of *great* wine.

And to merely exist is not to be great.

So-called 'alternative' varieties are too often celebrated in what I find to be a pointless manner—celebrated very often by small producers and way too often by some members of the media and frequently by some members of the trade for no reason other than they're different. Tastings reveal many are certainly not celebrated on the basis of quality.

And, no, Max Allen I am *not* talking about you; you are leading by example here and you are, through the Australian Alternative Varieties Wine Show and all your various outlets, providing important critical benchmarking for varietal exploration. We thank you.

But what we see very often is that the lesser producers in a region (and I'm talking Australia here) fail to make wine of sufficient quality in that region's most established/famous/successful/important/celebrated styles and so take refuge in obscurity as a means of staying out of a competition they cannot win. It's a game of attracting attention by alternative means and you can't really blame them.

I also see the same thing happen with wine writers; many a story has been written (and published) on the basis that something is different/new and therefore exciting/newsworthy. And I think it's a waste of precious publishing space when so much of what's really important is ignored in the name of an easy story that takes little time/effort/intellect to write. Editors often have bloodstained hands, too.

Imagine if investment writers wrote about companies simply on the basis that they were new and unproven in the market and they recommended it would be fun to try them. Would you be sinking your precious dollars in? Or if restaurant critics wrote up the new local restaurant because it's, well, new? Would you not want to know if the food is any good, the service and (more importantly perhaps) the wine list?

We all like to hear what's new, but I don't think that's enough when wine is at hand. Very few people have enough money to spend on wine to chance buying bad bottles simply on the basis that it's hardly been heard of, let alone perfected.

Wine critics are supposed to know enough to put all these millions of bottles into a useful context and to share their insight, their knowledge and experience. Ideally it's done with some wisdom, wit and generous spirit. Ditto sommeliers and wine merchants.

I don't want to just know that a wine is new or alternative; I want to know if it's any good. I also want to know why it's of interest, why it should be grown in one place and not another, why it is/will be great, how it delivers a profound result, and so on.

Every year I taste so many wines being made in Australia that are failed missions off along the tangent of new, alternative and different. Many are around for a few vintages only to gather dust in drab cellar-door bargain bins and be offered by online auction and discount wine specialists. What is the point? It's a waste of glass for starters.

If critics don't elucidate the good from the bad, if sommeliers and wine merchants don't make informed choices on the basis of an astute palate and wines are recommended and sold simply because they're weird/new/unheard of, we're proliferating a burgeoning lake of bad wine and—even worse than that—average wine.

It's a bit like those slightly corked bottles; most people can't identify the actual problem, they spend precious money, have a bad/unsatisfactory experience and go elsewhere. That's not going to end well for Australian wine.

Many 'alternative variety' wines simply shouldn't be bottled, let alone written about, listed and foisted upon unsuspecting consumers in the name of 'difference'—and this brings me to Paul Starr's final sentence: 'My knowledge is less than "expert" in wine or in Italian wine, and suspect it will always be the case that there is more left to learn than I will ever know. And I think I'd rather share my learning than my expertise, whatever size this pond is.'

Bravo. The great and frustrating allure of wine is that it is so diverse, so vast, newly minted every year and then changing constantly once bottled. It excites the hell out of me that great wines are being made all over the world as I write and as you read. There's so much to learn and so much learning to share.

But good winemakers—the ones who are successful, the ones we need, the ones who contribute to the culture of their region and the ones who are shaping the dynamic and exciting frontier that is Australian wine currently—are recognised because they make, bottle and release *great* wine.

Sharing your learning is one thing; bottling it in liquid form and asking people to part with their money to experience it is another game all together. You'll survive for a while making average wine in Australia (probably on the WET tax methadone program), but not for long.

Australia is at one very important crossroads as a wine-producing nation and we need everyone making the very best wine they can. One important piece of that puzzle is making educated, smart and sometimes tough decisions about what grape varieties to work with.

It's time to step up with courage and make distinctive wine, not just *any* wine. We need to be focused. And, frankly, we also need collective strategy to really succeed. And we need regions as well placed as the Canberra District to really nail it to the wall.

Great winemakers are those who don't bottle and release anything less than their very best. They don't put their name to anything that's average and they certainly don't do things on the basis of *vive la difference* first, quality second.

They showcase the results of detailed, thoughtful and astute experiments, the bounty of their hard work, their dedication, their clever intuition and, perhaps most importantly, their honest and self-effacing reflection. They proudly bottle concisely resolved results, not the experiment itself. Imagine the same with food. We wouldn't waste time eating the stuff.

And, as I said the other day in Canberra, just because you can, certainly doesn't mean you should. When I celebrate something, I like to celebrate with a glass of something great, not just something weird and wet.

15. The Search for Consistency or the Pursuit of Excellence? Single vineyard, regional and multi-regional as winemaking choices in Australia[1]

Brian Walsh
Yalumba

Excellence and Consistency are Not Mutually Exclusive

I am changing the subtheme, 'The search for consistency *or* the pursuit of excellence', to 'the search for consistency *and* the pursuit of excellence'.

Is it better to have an average wine from an exceptional single site or an outstanding wine from a combination of sites? And who decides?

In this room I suggest that many of us are interested principally in the intrinsic qualities, provenance and integrity of the wine, whatever the source(s); however, many or most wine purchasers might not have enough confidence in understanding or defining their own interpretation of high quality and look to 'experts' from many quarters for advice and validation.

I do not intend to talk for or against single sites, or multi-sites, or multi-regions, as if there was only one true way.

This is not a religion.

I intend to explore the positives and negatives of these winemaking philosophies with an overriding assumption that everyone involved in the creation of fine wine in Australia is trying to make wines of excellence.

---

[1] This paper was first delivered at Landmark Tutorial 2010, in the Yarra Valley, Victoria, with the 'allocated' title 'Single vineyard, regional and multi-regional as winemaking choices in Australia. A discussion about Australia's finest wines and the philosophy that surrounds its production. The search for consistency or the pursuit of excellence?'

Proceedings of the 7th University House Wine Symposium

What is Fine Wine?

In trying to define 'fine wine', it is difficult to not mention price per bottle.

That said, for all sorts of supply–demand reasons there are some high-end prices generally beyond the reach of a normal, genuine wine lover who might be on the 'average wage', and the disparity between the top-priced wine from Burgundy, Bordeaux, Stellenbosch, Piedmont, Margaret River, Oregon or the Canberra District is such that establishing a fair global comparison is difficult.

Perhaps rather than price, it is the top-valued 5 or 10 per cent of any major wine-producing region or nation?

Andrew Jefford suggested in January 2010 that, in Europe at least, fine wine represented less than 5 per cent of total production.

I suggest we don't get too prescriptive and definitely not too exclusive, as I am aware of many winemakers who are trying to make, and achieving success in making, fine wine at modest selling prices.

It is fair to say that we are excluding from this discussion those wines that generally sell below A$10 equivalent, as important to our collective futures as those wines are.

Wine Intelligence UK (May 2010)—not without some controversy—suggested that £10+, US$25+ and Swiss CHF25+ formed a logical line in the sand for fine wine.

A group of unnamed 'connoisseurs' was outraged, suggesting that they 'would not describe anything below £30 as fine wine'!

A subsequent *Wine Intelligence UK* consumer survey reported in June 2010 on consumers' expectations of fine wine.

Consumers valued: heritage, provenance, handcrafting, critical acclaim, family history and rarity.

Of particular interest was that the dimension of time was also important.

Consumers wanted to feel that

- time had been dedicated to the growing and making of the wine
- retailers and/or sommeliers will devote some time to assist in their decision making
- they made time available to drink the wine and cherish the experience.

I like that approach, where the winemaker takes time to craft a great wine and the wine drinkers make time to savour the wine. Very civilised!

Great Wine Does Not Start in the Vineyard

Contrary to the above widespread and popular belief, I assert that great wine starts in the brain.

The creation of fine wine is, at its source, an intellectual exercise. Someone has a dream, a vision, a hunch—then the desire, commitment, capability and energy to craft something special, typically with a desire for unique attributes that differentiate it from others.

There are admiration and inspiration emanating from other wines, but at the root there is a desire to create 'differentness'.

An Irony of the Taste of Terroir

During my working life in wine in Australia, I have often heard—and I have often said myself, generally in a positive sense—that a certain Australian wine has a *Rhone*-like character, in the case of a cool-region Shiraz, or is reminiscent of *Champagne*, in the case of a fine Australian sparkling, or has a hint of *Bordeaux*, in the case of a Coonawarra or Margaret River Cabernet.

Those comments imply that the more a wine is thought to show Old-World quality, style and flavour characteristics, the more we tend to praise it.

Apparently, as it loses some of its Australian-ness or local terroir, we admire it more. And often in the same breath we praise the apparent terroir influence on these fine wines—wines that have lost their Australian terroir and taken on the terroir characteristics of another place.

Andrew Jefford repeats the theme in 'Mateship with place', in Issue 28 of the *World of Fine Wine*. While referencing 30 fine Australian wines, he speaks of

- 'classy Shiraz in the Northern Rhone idiom, full of Yarra freshness'
- 'a palate of almost Burgundian purity'
- '…makes this the Mersault among Australian chardonnays'.

Terroir Gained or Terroir Lost?

Perhaps this is part of an Australian cultural cringe, as we have long had a habit of looking abroad for validation of our skills and expertise—and not just in wine, but in almost all forms of the arts.

Matt Kramer (*Wine Spectator*, 31 May 2008) argues that Old World/New World delineation is both increasingly more difficult and also less meaningful, not only qualitatively, but also increasingly stylistically.

My extrapolation of that position is that with tens of thousands of winegrowers around the world working on, by and large, the same dozen or so *Vitis vinifera* varieties, there will be countless wines that taste much the same and so the intimate, finite, measurable, explainable and supportable single vineyard will be an additional if not *the* additional attribute that creates long-term value for its owner/guardian.

In the same article, Kramer uses 'site deference' as a substitute for terroir, citing site deference as a mentality rather than a locality.

Steve Weber and Leanne De Bortoli go one further with their brand Riorret (*terroir* backwards, or is that down under?), the philosophy of which is 'wine with place and imagination'.

It is interesting that in 1991, more than 50 years after the formal foundation of the AOC system, Fanet said 'we are still very far away from being able to explain for each of the approximately 400 French Appellations, which of the characteristics of their terroir creates the originality and specificity of their wines'!

When is Consistency Good and When is it Bad?

In short, common current belief measured in terms of 'CCIWAs' (column centimetres in wine articles) is that consistency is bad when it happens in a winery and not in a vineyard.

Good winegrowers around the world

- choose planting material for consistent results or complementarity if mixed clones
- prune for consistency of crop
- manage canopy for consistency of exposure
- farm for consistency of vigour and vine health

- include selective stress
- shoot or bunch thin for consistency and placement of crop
- selectively pick for consistency of maturity
- after picking, sort for consistency of 'quality' or 'purity', as defined.

Generally, those actions are all deemed appropriate, whereas the next stage of intervention for consistency and higher quality—particularly in recent times—is sometimes and in some quarters seen as a negative or unnatural intrusion.

What is Natural and Unnatural?

It seems today that almost any 'winemaking', as in plying the winemaker's trade, is often seen as somewhat unnatural or interfering with nature.

The use of cultured yeast, acidification, filtration and now even microbiological stability is deemed unnatural. While overuse of any of those techniques can be intrusive, we should not abandon all the positive historical advances we have made in an ideological quest for natural.

Champagne and sherry, for example, would both be particularly difficult to make without good intervention and management of the processes.

In Australia we had potentially devastating problems with *Brettanomyces* as recently as 10 years ago, as, with good intentions, we moved to a lower sulfur dioxide regime without thinking of past lessons learned.

In much of Australia in the 2011 vintage, lack of intervention would have meant total loss.

It is disappointing to read the following statements.

Jacques Lardiere, head winemaker at Louis Jadot, in *Decanter* (September 2010), said:

> [W]ineries that clean up their wines are removing the life from them.
>
> I'm not after technical perfection. I don't have much time for the Australian approach, where the ideal wine is the most neutral.
>
> It's easy to clean up a wine, but by removing faults, *unless they are truly detrimental*, you also remove its life. (Emphasis added)

Most of us would not disagree with Lardiere that in fine wine a hint of 'wildness' is not a bad thing, but there is a dangerous fine line to be walked and it is incorrect to assert that Australia's ideal wine is our most neutral.

There is a fair chance that Lardiere might not have been exposed to a huge selection of Australia's Landmark wines.

There is a certain inconsistency in growing the finest grapes possible and then allowing (encouraging?) faults to develop with little care or concern.

Tim White (*Australian Financial Review*, 13–15 August 2010) provided another view that essentially says that if we take naturalness to its logical conclusion, we would not be making wine in Australia from imported vine stock at all: 'the way we cultivate the vine is about as unnatural as it gets', noting that in its natural habitat it is a climber of trees and other conveniently accessible objects.

He then goes further: 'if we follow the notion of "naturalness" as it applies on this continent we should not be making wine out of the grapes of *Vitis vinifera* at all, given that it is an introduced species.'

I raise the issues of consistency and naturalness as I sense in recent times the concept of terroir has been too narrowly attributed to place—to the exclusion of philosophy and people.

The following is Warren Moran's translation of the INAO's notes on terroir in 2000:

> A social construction within a natural space gifted with homogeneous characteristics, delimited on the cadastra, and characterised by a set of values—aesthetic landscape values, cultural values of historical significance, patrimonial values of social significance and values related to its reputation.

Moran (Christchurch, NZ, 2006) talks of the six facets of terroir—agro, vini, territorial, identity, legal and promotional—highlighting the absolute need for human intervention.

Our History of Blending

In Australia

Interregional

As noted by Brian Croser at the Landmark Tutorial 2009, much of the 'golden era' of interregional blending—the 1940s to 1960s—was based on curiosity, experimentation and genuinely trying to make a better wine, keeping in mind also that the production of dry table wine was a very small part of our commercial wine industry.

Importantly it is also implied that its origins were in 'mateship' or industry camaraderie, which grew into the swapping, trading and subsequent blending of a cask or two of each other's wines.

There is also the possibility that in that very process of blending, these winemakers were questioning whether some of the attributes that their mates' wines were bringing to the equation might be reproducible closer to home.

In many cases this might have been a conscious or subconscious search for single sites.

Certainly in the case of Roger Warren of Hardy's, he was not convinced of the quality of McLaren Vale Shiraz for red table wine, leading to a search further afield for other blending options—the pursuit of excellence.

In my early days in wine in Australia (the late 1960s), the Barossa–Coonawarra blends of Penfolds' Max Schubert, the Hunter–McLaren Vale or Tahbilk–McLaren Vale blends of Hardy's Roger Warren, the Hunter–Coonawarras of Mildara and others were the stuff of legend. We were, and still are, very proud of those wines, although as we seem to be inexorably driven towards single sites as the pinnacle of our craft, we are today less likely to try to emulate these great wines. Bravo to Penfolds for the strengths of its brands, giving it the capacity and confidence to continue with a long list of superb interregional wines.

In that era (1940s to 1970s), the pursuit of excellence could be argued as the pursuit and purchase of the wine, not the pursuit and purchase of the land to grow the wine and definitely not the search for a single site.

Andrew Jefford (Personal communication) said that one could argue that this interregional blending of fine wine could be considered as one form of Australian terroir—a multi-terroir.

Of Varieties

Varietal labelling became the fashion from the late 1960s and into the 1970s in Australia, modelled somewhat on the Californian experience. Hitherto our wines had generally been labelled as Claret, Burgundy, Champagne, Hock, Graves and the list goes on.

For some not easily or logically explainable reason, for the next 30 years or so, single varietal wines were generally deemed—in the marketplace—to be superior to 'blended wines'.

Blends assumed a blending down rather than a blending up in quality.

Is it possible that in another generation we might be having the same discussion about single vineyards (in lieu of single varietals) and blended vineyards (in lieu of blends of varieties) and again be questioning the logic?

In the days of Clarets and Burgundies, blending of varieties was quite common. Shiraz, Grenache, Carignane, Oeillade and Cabernet Sauvignon were generally made without reference to the varieties.

Were we more or less sophisticated then? The variety wasn't that important, just the maker and the wine.

When red wine boomed there was some blending down, with Grenache converted from fortified to table wine production. It helped give Grenache a bad name, not that it was the grape's fault; it was the fault of the winemakers.

But the blending up continued and as our winemakers looked for a Cabernet blender they chose Shiraz. It was in abundance and the synergies, the yin and yang, with Cabernet Sauvignon proved extremely successful.

In about 1865 Dr Jules Guyot, philosopher, scientist and oenological adviser, recommended adding Syrah to Cabernet to the producers in Provence, but to the best of my knowledge the recommendation wasn't taken up with gusto.

The Bordelaise practised 'hermitaging' before it was legislated out of order.

Would Bordeaux have been better in say the 1970s and 1980s if 'hermitaging' was still permitted and practised? Chateau Palmer, in a quite expensive *vin de table*, has begun revisiting 'hermitaging'.

How lucky were we in Australia to be able to assume a world leadership position with this great blend?

Within Regions

This was and is the most common activity, where large, medium and some small wineries carefully choose grapes from within their region or subregion, knowing that ultimately many will go together into the final wine and hoping for complementarity of flavours and textures.

Maurice O'Shea, one of Australia's greatest winemakers, was noted for his ability to select complementary parcels of wine from neighbours to craft outstanding Hunter reds. My understanding is that often this was wine not grapes.

That skill was practised also in the 1970s and later by a young Wolfgang Blass, with great commercial success, although in a sign of the times, Blass was disparaged by some as 'just' a blender—not a term that was used to describe Maurice O'Shea.

Warren Moran at Terroir 2006 (UC Davis) said that 'to assemble wines from different terroirs is little different from assembling different varieties in the same terroir'—a version of Andrew Jefford's multi-terroir?

Is not a multi-site wine from within a single or multiple geographic indication merely a blend of several single sites?

Vintage Champagne is one of the finest examples of multi-cuvees from within a large region—generally aimed at raising the quality bar.

What is a Single Vineyard and Why is it Important?

It is my view that the single vineyard is an arbitrary construct.

One could argue that one of the reasons for a single-site approach to winemaking *is* to show consistency over time from a single source, not withstanding that nature intervenes to provide the variations induced by seasonality.

However, we cannot and should not avoid acknowledging the intellectual property values in a defined site and how that has the potential to create serious and well-justified wealth in the correct hands.

If most of what the collective winemakers of the world do in terms of practices and techniques is to be copied, it is ultimately only the site that cannot be truly copied by another—even if the result is very similar.

There is currently no definition of a single site in our Australian wine law, but common law would imply a clearly defined vineyard of known boundaries, most likely a contiguous piece of land and possibly under single ownership.

A single vineyard or farm may not be claimed under US wine law unless 95 per cent of the fruit comes from that vineyard.

Recently the South African wine producers defined single vineyards. A key point was that a single vineyard may not be greater than 6 ha in size. Is this driven by an assumption that if greater than 5 ha, homogeneity of the land might be corrupted (less consistency?), or is it driven by an assumption that smaller (and more exclusive) is a better marketing fit for a consumer expectation of single site?

Noteworthy also is that a single-vineyard wine may only be planted to a single variety. What *are* they thinking?

Proceedings of the 7th University House Wine Symposium

The Irony of the Single Vineyard

A single vineyard implies homogeneity of soil and climate. It implies a single terroir of reproducible consistency.

The search for consistency by other means is seen by some as a dumbing down, not an enriching experience.

In reality, most single sites will have some degree of variability within the boundaries of the vineyard: soil structure and depth, available moisture content, subtle changes in elevation or exposure to the elements.

A single vine is the ultimate, yet totally impractical expression of a unique terroir.

Some great single vineyards are planted on slopes where we know there is a difference between top, middle and bottom, due to soil depth, fertility, temperature, sunlight interception and so on. This reinforces the variability within a single vineyard, arguing against the aim of homogeneity.

As an aside, Brian Croser notes in 'My pinosity' (*The World of Fine Wine*, 2009) another apparent paradox, where in the pursuit of fine wine, we tend to choose the coolest possible region and then select the warmest possible site on which to plant. I don't think he posed the next question of should we find a warm region and choose the coldest possible site?

Our History of Single Sites

Australia has a long history of single-site wines, although I sense we tend (with notable exceptions) not to celebrate them with the same degree of reverence that we might a European single vineyard of real stature—and maybe that's reasonable. We should respect history and heritage as intrinsic parts of wine culture and be patient in waiting for greatness to be bestowed.

The shorter-term challenge for those of us with single-vineyard programs is to articulate what this means to our domestic and international audiences.

Beyond the classic Australian single-site wines, many of which you will have tasted, there is an emerging class of new single sites, providing a very exciting development for us all.

While I expect this is happening across many Australian wine regions, I will talk about the Barossa project, due to knowledge of, and familiarity with, the project.

The Barossa Ground project is a collaborative exercise being undertaken by the winegrowers of the Barossa to see (initially over a five-year period) whether and how the different soil types, aspects and microclimates of the Barossa, as they apply to Shiraz, can be transferred into the wines and how that knowledge can be accumulated, interpreted and articulated to the wider wine community.

As a by-product of the process, many more significant and distinguished vineyard sites are being isolated and will most likely come onto market as single-site offerings.

So much of the value in single-site winemaking is in the focused search for perfection and the associated accumulation of site-specific knowledge and information. It certainly represents one aspect of 'the pursuit of excellence'.

Conclusion

Excellence and consistency are not mutually exclusive.

Single vineyard, regional and multi-regional are winemaking choices for Australian winegrowers.

Many great fine wines have been and will continue to be made from those choices.

Vive la difference!

As the boundaries of individuality and uniqueness, of Old World and New World become blurred, the single site is one incontestable protection of intellectual property.

Winegrowers without a single site must carefully develop their own differentiation capability and a method for communicating their story.

Consistency is not inherently bad; consistently great is a worthy ambition.

Winemaking intervention, with knowledge, care and sensitivity, should not be scorned.

www.ingramcontent.com/pod-product-compliance
Lightning Source LLC
Chambersburg PA
CBHW060947170426
43197CB00031B/2995